D1370591

Landscape Design . . . Texas Style

Landscape Design ...Texas Style

HOWARD GARRETT

Foreword by
Stanley Marcus

Taylor Publishing Company

Dallas, Texas

Library of Congress Cataloging-in-Publication Data

Garrett, Howard.
   Landscape design — Texas style.

   Includes index.
   1. Landscape architecture — Texas. 2. Landscape gardening — Texas. 3.
Gardens — Texas — Design. 4. Gardens — Texas — Pictorial works. I.
Title.
SB472.32.U6G37   1986   712′.09764   86-1871
ISBN 0-87833-524-2

Editorial Consultation: Kim Lively

Book Design: Tina Forster

Printed in the United States of America

9 8 7 6 5 4 3 2 1

To my parents
Ruby and Jewell Garrett

Contents

"Landscaping is not a complex and difficult act to be practiced only by high priests. It is logical, down-to-earth, and aimed at making your plot of ground produce exactly what you want and need from it. What you will have, I hope, is a garden more beautiful than you had anticipated, with less care than you had expected, and costing only a little more than you had planned."

Gardens Are For People
Thomas Church, 1955

Foreword

Landscape Design . . . Texas Style is a landscaping book and gardening guide for Texas residents. It's about Texas climate, plants that will grow in the various regions of Texas, and those that won't. It's also about the hard-construction elements of garden design. This book is not filled with armchair observations; rather, it is the result of a personal tour of Texas by the author to observe firsthand what grows well and what doesn't in the major population areas of our state.

From the vast number of how-to books on the market, it seems that there are authorities on every subject. Almost all cooks appear to have confidence to write about cooking, but reading through their cookbooks, it becomes obvious that cooking capability does not necessarily go pot in hand with the ability to write.

Recipes must be in specific definable terms, timing must be stated in exact numbers, and all recipes must be thoroughly tested, preferably by someone other than the author.

The same caveats apply to writing about landscaping and gardening. Being a successful gardener or a professional writer is not enough. A writer in this field must not only have mastered the subjects, but he must have an orderly, logical mind, a keen sense of perception, and a willingness to travel the territory; otherwise, he must be content to write about the topic from a local single-county perspective.

Garrett has developed a new type of climate zone map which looks much more accurate than the ones with which I have been familiar. He has made easy-to-read, separate listings of the various trees, shrubs, ground covers, flowers, vines, and grasses that grow in each zone. The names of the major cities are noted in each area designation so there can be no opportunity for confusion or obfuscation.

As a rank amateur, I find that I can understand what he's writing about without further explanation. I have a clearer understanding of my plant options, I have a better idea of how to prune, and I have a more sophisticated appreciation of the philosophy of landscaping as well as of the author's own credo.

This is an easy-to-read book, partially because the author expresses his opinions clearly and without equivocation and partially because the illustrative material is so accurately keyed to the copy. It's an informative book for the serious landscape expert; it is a stimulating guide for the amateur. It's the kind of book that would be fun even on a bumpy airplane trip, for it's fascinating to decipher the vegetation and tree material that will grow in your own garden.

Probably the best previous book on landscaping has been *Gardens Are For People* by Thomas Church, the illustrious landscape designer of the San Francisco Bay area. That was a general book for all sections of the country. Now, *Landscape Design . . . Texas Style* is a book just for Texans. The rest of the U.S. is going to be jealous.

A Word About How to Use This Book

Whether you are a do-it-yourselfer or someone looking for professional help, this book is for those homeowners, architects, and developers who want to learn about landscape architecture and how to accomplish it in Texas. The instruction given in this book, just like the teaching methods used in golf, skiing, and other sports, as well as most other arts, encourages learning by association from visual images. *Landscape Design . . . Texas Style* gives hundreds of specific design ideas that can be applied to a variety of projects. Even though the projects shown vary widely in size and budget, the design principles can apply to gardens of any size.

Using this book is very easy. Part I, INTRODUCTION TO DESIGN, explains landscape architecture and presents my personal philosophy of design. This section gives you a good basis of information needed to be comfortable with the design portion of a project.

Part II, DESIGNING YOUR OWN PROJECT, explains the design process and illustrates how it works by taking an actual project step by step through the process.

Part III, INSTALLING YOUR LANDSCAPE, discusses the ins and outs of hard construction and planting. It also covers specific plant materials, and hard-construction details, ranging from edgings and steps to terraces and fences. Photos show these details used in actual settings, and the text explains their purposes and best uses.

Part IV, MAINTAINING YOUR LANDSCAPE, not only covers simple, practical maintenance instructions, but also gives instruction on maintenance as a design tool.

Part V, CASE STUDIES, consists of 38 case studies of actual projects our firm has designed and completed in Texas. These projects range widely in scale, budget, and character. You will notice similar elements in some of them, but little pattern as to look or style. Each project is customized to a particular site and for an individual client. Readers can use this section to learn how particular problems are solved and adapt specific design ideas to their own properties. Although some of the projects shown are large, the design concepts of specific plant massings, courtyards, and details can be used on any size garden space.

Residential design work is covered most extensively in the following pages, but some commercial projects are included to show how the same design principles apply to both. People with smaller properties will be able to benefit the most from this book because the variety of design ideas shown allows the homeowner to use similar ideas in his own garden space without the huge expense of a large project.

Special Thanks

My wife tolerates my obsessions more than anyone. Judy, pregnant with our daughter, Logan, during the completion of the book was the first to help. She had great thoughts on what to write in general, and how to express it to the public; she also did much of the early editing. She scheduled and booked my trips around Texas and patiently accepted the time we spent creating and producing the book.

Alan Abé not only continued to run HGA, but was invaluable in the structure, writing, final editing, and the photography of the book. Additional thanks go to Kathy, his wife, and sons Brian and Kevin for their understanding of the time it took us to finish the book.

Mike Boydston was crucial to the successful completion of the book because he kept all of our design projects under control during their construction. He also assisted with the construction and plant material parts of the book and the final editing.

Mark Sockwell, my administrative assistant, not only kept my schedule and managed the administrative staff, but spent many long hours typing all of the book from rough drafts to the final text and helped with the editing.

Susan Klein kept the design stages of HGA projects under control, managed numerous projects, and directed the production of the drawings and sketches for the book.

Lee Roth continued to manage several design projects, coordinated all the photographic sessions for the case studies, and assisted with the photography.

Russell Haas also managed several HGA design projects, while producing some of the graphics for the book.

Kevin Starnes, Leah Green, David Samuelson, Greg Stevens, Mike Wineinger, and Laura Shehan all contributed considerably by cheerfully working on HGA design projects and the book by doing research with people around the state, preparing sketches and drawings, helping with the photography, and generally keeping our design business going.

Friends and colleagues from around the state who helped with their suggestions and advice include: Black's Nursery in El Paso; Jerry Lewis in El Paso; Gerald Rhodes at Currie's Landscaping in Corpus Christi; Randy Rogers of Blue Heron Designs, Inc. in Midland and San Antonio; Len Newsom in Midland; the parks department in Amarillo; Jud Gilliland of the Four Seasons Landscape Co. in Abilene; Curtis Tabor of Southwest Landscape Nursery Co., Inc. in Dallas; Ross Ayers with Cornelius Nurseries, Inc. in Houston; Lynn and Nancy Wilkinson in Abilene; Rob and Jerilyn Nalley in Houston; Lt. Col. Joe and Lou Howard in Austin; Tom Keeter in San Antonio; Otto Scherz in San Angelo; and John Morelock of Seasonal Colour Garden Shoppe in Dallas.

Kim Lively was hired by Taylor Publishing Company to work with us during the final month of writing to help clean up some of my language and pull from me the information I assumed everyone already knew. Thanks go to Taylor Publishing Company for the successful production and marketing of the book. Most helpful were Arnie Hanson, Freddie Goff, Kathy Ferguson, Carol Buch, and Annette Schmidt.

Sincere thanks go to cover artist Lee Hendricks, and book designer Tina Forster.

Landscape Design . . . Texas Style is a pictorial garden tour. Names and addresses of most of the residential owners have been omitted to protect their privacy. However, these homeowners have been very helpful with the creation of this book by allowing their gardens to be published in these pages, and I would like to thank them very sincerely.

And finally, many thanks to my friend Stanley Marcus for his encouragement and advice.

I. *Introduction to Design*

What Is Landscape Architecture?

Over the past 12 years my staff and I have spent many hours attempting to define the term landscape architecture. The process is much easier than the definition. Having beaten this question to death, we have come up with the following explanation:

Landscape architecture is the design of outdoor space and its elements.

Contrary to popular opinion, the selection and location of plants is just one of the facets of landscape architecture. In some projects there may be no plants used at all, just the location of buildings, sculpture, paths, terraces, water, etc.

In the creation of spaces, the look is important, but the quality of the feel of the place is the most important. For example, in our gardens, we don't want people to say, "This is pretty," but instead, "I enjoy being here and want to come back."

Landscape architecture involves thousands of tasks, but the most important one may be the ability of the designer not only to look at the existing landscape, but also to observe and listen to the owners. It seems that the most successful design solutions have resulted from a very strong collaboration between the designer and the people who will be using the project.

Conversely, the most unsuccessful projects are those where the designer goes into a corner and designs something that pleases him greatly due to its graphic wherewithal. The result is a project that falls miserably short in interest or usefulness when built. Along the same lines, when a homeowner designs a garden, he or she must observe and address his or her own landscape needs and desires in detail before beginning the work.

The practice of landscape architecture is relatively young in the Southwest, but is rapidly approaching a serious level of sophistication. For people who would like to learn landscape architecture on a formal basis, many schools around the country have a wide variety of curricula. Four schools in Texas offer degree programs in landscape architecture or related fields. Richland College offers a two-year degree in landscape contracting and greenhouse management. UTA offers a master's degree in landscape architecture. A bachelor of science degree and a master's degree are available at Texas A&M, and a bachelor of science is offered at Texas Tech University.

I would recommend that anyone pursuing this field as a profession acquire as much basic formal education as possible. However, formal education in lieu of practical experience in the field would be a great mistake. Pursuing the two simultaneously or obtaining field experience immediately upon completion of formal schooling would be the best combination of educations.

My formal education at Texas Tech consisted of bouncing from one degree to the next and avoiding much of a complete background. Consequently, I had no choice but to learn the business in the field by working during college and then, after graduation, as a golf-course laborer and assistant superintendent. Although I graduated from Texas Tech University

with a bachelor of science degree in landscape architecture, my practical experience in the marketplace was my true education.

If you are considering some professional input on your landscaping, it is important to understand how to hire a landscape expert. Many people are intimidated by the idea and never get around to asking how the process works.

There are several kinds of landscape professionals and various ways to work with them. Generally speaking, landscape professionals organize their businesses into one of three broad categories:

Landscape Contractors

Good landscape contractors are organized business people with sophisticated methods of cost control, inventories, subcontractors, etc. These people bid and install the work designed by landscape architects and industrious homeowners. However, all it takes to become a landscape contractor is to have a pickup truck and the ability to convince someone to hire you. (Due to that fact, there are some real shysters in the business.)

Contractors have some design ability, but primarily concentrate their efforts on the contracting side of the business. They don't charge much, if anything, for design or consultation. Unless they are licensed with the state, contractors should not charge for the design, only the construction. (If you'd like to check a contractor's credentials, just ask to see his or her license. Better still, ask for a client reference list, and check it out.)

Design/Build Landscape Architects

These people design primarily in order to sell the landscape installation, although some companies have two distinct departments — design and construction. They usually charge for design, but the fees are reasonable for the average client. Again, the primary aim here is to sell the landscape installation. When dealing with these people, make sure you find out where their priorities lie.

Design/Only Landscape Architects

These people work for fees only and do no landscape installation. Fees are charged on an hourly basis, an agreed upon lump sum, or a percentage of the contract. These designers develop plans and specifications, recommend bidders, and oversee the construction in the field.

The State of Texas requires that people practicing landscape architecture be licensed by passing a test that covers site planning, design, professional practice, history, and plant materials. Unfortunately, there's not much enforcement of the law.

In addition, there are two landscape businesses that are primarily sellers of plant materials; their employees often dispense advice on recommended plant varieties, and their cultivation and care.

Wholesale Plant Growers grow landscape plant material for sale to landscape contractors and retail nurseries.

Retail Nurseries sell plant materials and other landscape products direct to the public.

One final definition: A "landscaper" is kind of like the boogeyman; there's no such thing!

My Philosophy of Design

My design philosophy has three basic parts. First, I believe that **accepted landscaping rules are made to be broken.** Creativity is much more important than following an established pattern. Second, **a garden design should be flexible,** allowing a landscape to mature gracefully from an exciting starting point. And third, **learning about landscape design is a continual process** of experimentation and adaptation.

Let's take a closer look at each of these three basic ideas. First, a significant part of my design philosophy is that existing rules are not very good in many cases. Throughout this book, you will encounter unconventional landscape theories involving design and construction details. Hopefully, you will see that many of the conventional rules of landscaping are more myth than fact; these myths are still around simply because they've been perpetuated by word-of-mouth or laziness.

The following are some of my unconventional, rule-breaking ideas (that probably won't be unusual in another 10 years).

Trees are more important than all other landscape design elements put together. One of the reasons is a tree's endurance. Shrubs and flowers just don't live for 300 years. Some trees *do* — and with proper planting and care, they become more beautiful and valuable every year. If a budget is limited or has to be cut, cut anything but the trees. A landscape of just trees and grass is hard to beat.

Great amounts of money are wasted on unnecessary bed preparation. Some plant materials require extensive bed preparation while other plants require none. Preparing all beds the same way usually results in overkill — providing expensive treatment for plants that don't need it. Many people overtreat simply because they don't understand the specific needs of each plant in their landscape.

Maintenance is a design element. My favorite projects are those using existing plant materials. The protection, trimming, and selective removal of certain plants is the kind of design that results in the best project — one that doesn't appear to have been designed. The correct pruning of existing trees may be *the* most important and powerful design tool.

Designing a garden to one particular style is silly. Romanesque, Italian Renaissance, Post Modern, who cares? Design should be a composite expression of the site, the owner, and the designer. That the design works is the key. Landscape design is an art, and new forms of expression in art far outweigh copying someone else's design or adhering to one particular style or time period.

Also key to my philosophy is the second basic idea, that garden designs should be flexible. Don't worry about making changes occasionally. This is especially true in residential landscape design. My own home gardens have changed many times through the years because I am always trying new ideas and new plant materials. Thinning your landscape — removing certain plants completely — is a good idea from time to time. This allows the other materials more room to breathe and grow.

Making such plant material alterations is not only exciting, it is necessary from time to time. For example, in many new gardens, the lack of mature trees allows ample full sun for flowering plants, but these plants will have to be replaced with shade-loving plants as the trees grow and mature.

If you want to create a successful landscape, keep in mind its short and long-term aspects. When designing, always consider the garden's immediate impact as well as how the garden will look 40 years from now. After all, you want to start enjoying your beautiful outdoor environment as soon as possible, but you also want it to mature gracefully and improve with age.

My third basic belief, that landscape design is a continual learning experience, is crucial: those who think they have figured it all out are doomed to mediocrity. I think everyone should experiment with alternate possibilities and new ideas.

The way to start experimenting is very simple; get something on paper as quickly as possible. Sitting and thinking about design does very little good. As soon as you've sketched something, no matter whether it is good or bad, the editing and refining process can begin. A lot of your rough drafts may end up in the trash can. You may have to start over several times, but at least you will have begun. I cannot overemphasize how important it is to get something down on paper so the critiquing and editing process can begin. Don't be afraid to admit an idea stinks, and to try something else.

If you're intimidated by the prospect of making that first sketch, try to envision your landscape as if it were a room in your home. Draw your first landscape sketch just like a floor plan, then, instead of furniture and accessories, arrange the drawing with the placement of plants and hard-scape materials. Substitute grass for the floor, ground cover for area rugs, specimen shrubs for lamps and coffee tables, sidewalks for halls, vines for walls, tree canopies for ceilings, and ornamental trees for floor lamps.

The following illustrations will give you an idea of how to use this tool.

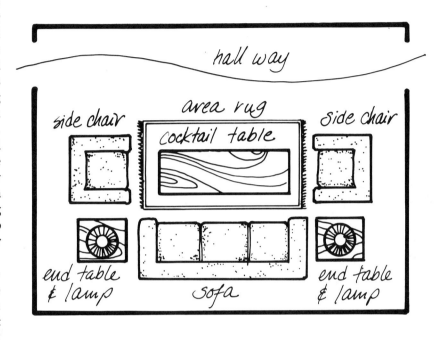

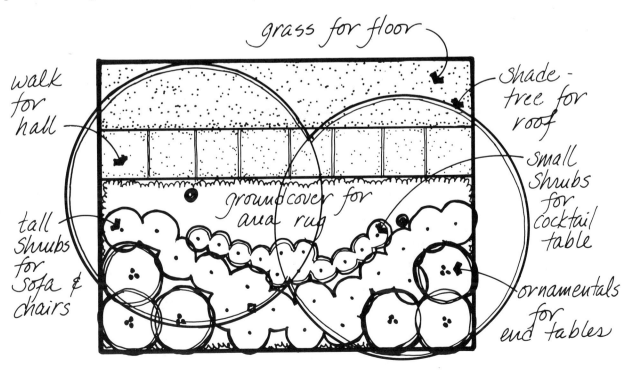

Another good way to begin a design is to borrow an idea from nature or from another landscape setting and try to make it better. Every good design doesn't have to be a totally new one. Even world-renowned artists employ this technique.

I once visited the studio of famed English sculptor, Henry Moore. He strongly believes in borrowing the form of some natural object for his new creations. In fact, during my visit he was shaping a hand-held model using an animal bone for inspiration.

I noted, too, that Mr. Moore approaches conceptual design in a trial-and-error manner; even he throws away a lot of rough ideas that just don't work.

Remember: All the time you're trying out new ideas, you're learning more. At the beginning of a project, use a lot of different ideas. Massage the good ideas into better ones, and groom and improve hard details of the plan.

My first book, *Plants of the Metroplex*, is a fine example of learning by trial and error. The first edition, in 1975, was unintentionally humorous, with several errors. However, the second edition of the book is thorough, and a better reflection of my design philosophy.

Landscape design is a constantly challenging endeavor whose accepted rules should be constantly challenged through experimentation with flexible designs.

With all that philosophy duly noted, what do I consider *good* design? It is that which pleases the users of the space, inspires people to learn more about the environment they live in, and raises their sensitivity to the quality of things around them.

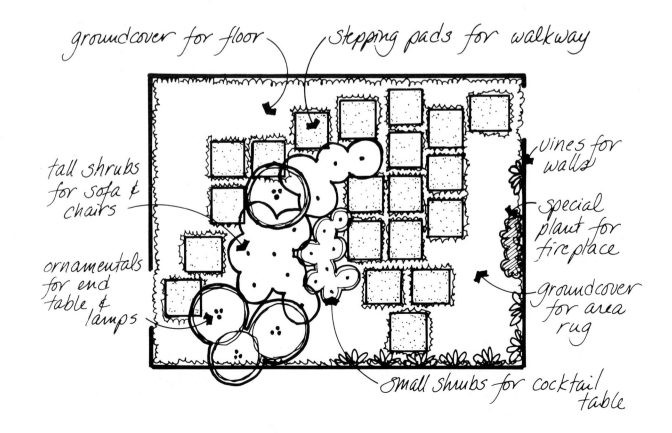

II. *Designing Your Own Project*

The Design Process

hether you are a homeowner or a landscape architect, this process is the same.

If you are lucky enough to be starting with a bare lot, this entire thought process can start at the optimum time, before any decisions have been made about siting the house and/or other structures.

A properly designed project is one where the architect, landscape architect, engineer, and owner work together from the very beginning, ideally, even before the site is selected.

Unfortunately, a large percentage of residential projects involve an existing house and other structures that prohibit designing the landscape and house at the same time.

Since a larger number of projects fall into this second category, that is the type of project that is taken through the step-by-step design process on the following pages. It is a real project owned by the W.C. Cole family in Dallas, Texas. (The process described, however, is the same for any city in the state.)

Pre-Design

Pre-design is the first step in the landscape-planning process. Many people skip this step and roar right into deciding on the placement of elements or even doing the actual installation. This is one of the most common mistakes in landscaping.

Pre-design is a term used to mean all those things that are done prior to the actual design. The following steps make up the pre-design portion of the landscape planning process.

1. WRITE THE PROGRAM

The program is the definition of a design problem and the parameters within which to solve it. It is a list of facts that are needed to be able to start the design.

Take a piece of paper and write down all the details about the project, including your entertainment and maintenance requirements, and your overall budget.

The Cole Program:

Owner: Mr. and Mrs. W. C. Cole

Location: A long, narrow lot in University Park

Children: 3 daughters: two married, one college-age who lives at home in summer.

Pets: 1 "inside" dog

Entertainment Requirements: Small parties often, large party no more than once per year.

Maintenance Requirements: Low. Wife prefers to work only with a small area of flowers.

General Notes: A duplex conversion to a single-family residence; will probably sell house within 10 years. Family owns several cars; parking is very tight.

2. SET THE BUDGET

How much you should spend on your landscaping is impossible to answer with cut-and-dried facts.

Of course, the best way to install any project is to do it all at one time. If budget money isn't available to do all the work at one time, the project should be broken down into phases, with money allotted to each phase.

The overall budget for the Cole landscape was $40,000, with $10,000 allotted to Phase 1.

A good, rough rule of thumb in regard to budgets is to allow approximately 10 to 20 percent of the property value for site improvement. Major amenities, such as pools and tennis courts, would be above and beyond the 10- to 20-percent budget.

The budget should be thought out not only in terms of Phase 1 costs, but also in terms of later phases and long-term maintenance costs.

The specific budget breakdown can most clearly be identified during the design development stage, when you have begun to select hard construction and plant materials, but an overall budget should be established in the beginning.

3. ESTABLISH THE SCHEDULE

It's very important to set the time frame for the project. For the Cole project, one month was allotted to design; three months were allotted to construction of Phase 1.

The ideal schedule is the following: Design the project in the spring and summer; install it in the fall and winter, and start enjoying it the following spring.

Planning to install a garden in the spring is what most people do, and that is the very worst time. Spring is when landscape professionals are busiest, and nursery stock is lowest, because the mad rush is on by so many homeowners who scheduled their landscaping poorly. If installation is done in the fall and winter, plants will develop some root growth during the dormant season, and take off growing vigorously in the spring.

4. OBTAIN A SURVEY OF THE EXISTING FEATURES

You should measure your property and make a drawing showing the existing features — property lines, fences, plant materials, easements; the drawing should be to scale (1"=8' for properties up to one acre in size, and 1"=20' for properties over one acre.) This will vary depending on the scope of the project, but is a good rule of thumb. Identifying the grades is also important to avoid or solve drainage problems.

On the Cole project, the grades are basically flat, making any improvement sensitive, meaning that any improvement done may cause problems with the existing plants and drainage. The grades at the base of the large existing pecan are important because cutting or filling in the root-system area can be detrimental to the tree.

5. PERFORM THE SITE ANALYSIS

Site analysis is the documentation on a drawing of the existing features of a site such as sun orientation, good and bad views, overhang of neighbors' trees, types of soils, etc. The design of the project begins at this point because observing and learning about existing features helps to visualize the use of those existing elements. The secret here is to use as many of the existing features as possible. Corrective maintenance procedures for existing plant materials should be noted at this time.

Performing a site analysis, which is simply a compilation of the existing features, is not enough. One has to understand the site and its trees, rock outcroppings, and water, etc., or lack thereof. Understanding why these given features exist provides important information about what can and cannot be built, and what can and cannot grow on the site.

SITE SURVEY

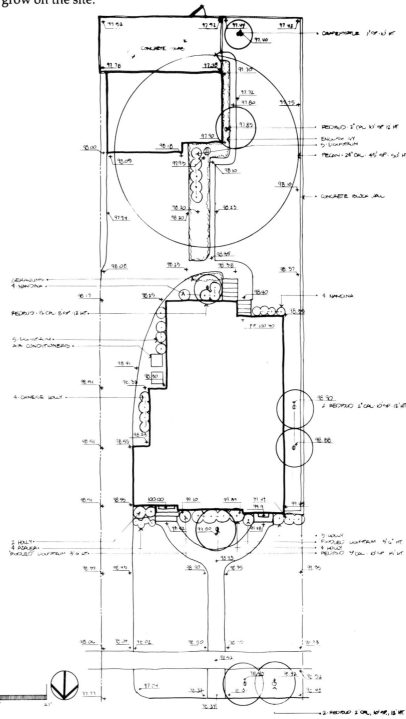

Understanding new construction materials and introduced plant materials is important, but understanding the soil and the existing plant life is even more critical.

6. IDENTIFY EARLY-ACTION MAINTENANCE REQUIREMENTS

Determine if existing trees need to be sprayed for insects or disease, pruned of dead or damaged limbs, or given supplemental water. If you do not feel competent to make these decisions alone, seek the help of someone knowledgeable; contractors,

nurserymen, or even some landscape architects can assist you.

In the Cole plan, the existing pecan tree in the back yard was the most critical factor. Because of the new construction, some roots were cut during early utility work on the house, so a few tree limbs had to be removed to compensate for the root loss. Extra watering of the tree was also necessary.

On all projects, especially small ones, it's difficult to keep construction traffic and materials away from the root systems of the trees. Keeping all foot and vehicular traffic off the root systems of trees during construction is ideal. If that isn't possible, keep it to a minimum. Literally erecting fences to keep people out is the best solution.

Okay, we're almost ready to start drawing, but first let me chat briefly about:

Designing for Low Maintenance

Maintenance-free gardens don't exist because gardens are living things that do not remain static. Even if they did, they would be very boring after the first few weeks. One of the most important features of any garden is its chameleonlike character — the fascinating way it changes through the seasons and the years.

It may seem strange to address the idea of maintenance in the middle of a design book, but as explained in the philosophy section, I feel that maintenance is a very important design tool. And if you want to create a low-maintenance landscape, you need to start thinking about this aspect as you consider your design.

Man's desire to get out and work on and in the land is very basic, but today's pressures and time restraints have reduced man's involvement with nature. The city dweller no longer digs, plows, and plants; he or she now only pulls an occasional weed or trims a broken or out-of-place limb (that is, if it is a small limb and low enough to reach while standing on the ground).

Most homeowners don't have time to do much more than that, hence the increasing popularity of low-maintenance landscapes. The homeowner needs to be able to get out and enjoy working in the garden,

SITE ANALYSIS

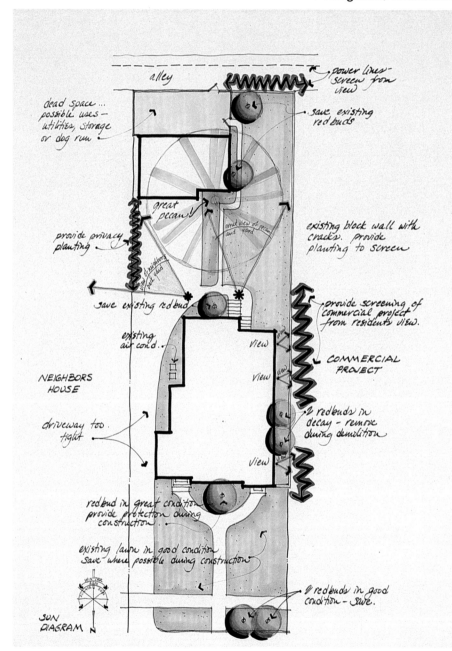

without feeling like he or she is fighting a losing battle against a never-ending army of weeds, hard soil, and all sorts of creatures and critters.

One of the best ways to ensure a low-maintenance landscape is by careful plant selections. Luckily, several dwarf varieties of plants are available now that will give a better effect, be healthier, and require much less trimming than the "parents" from which they were hybridized. Some of the best examples are dwarf Chinese holly, compact nandina, and dwarf yaupon holly.

During the past year, one of the biggest design mistakes I've seen has been the use of large areas of ground cover in an attempt to create low-maintenance landscapes. These primarily commercial installations cost a bundle, were impossible to establish, and now they are being mowed because the grasses and weeds took over. So, if you have large areas that need some planting — use grass. Large areas of ground cover are appropriate only on sites too shady for grass.

And now, you're ready to draw something!

Conceptual Design

This is a five-step drawing process. The first step is to define general spaces and specific use areas; second is the graphic definition of circulation routes; third is the refinement of the circulation system, showing the shape and size of the paving; locating the major trees is fourth; and drawing the final conceptual plan showing all the elements (hard construction and plants) is the fifth step.

1. DEFINITION OF GENERAL SPACES AND SPECIFIC USE AREAS

First of all, you need to define the spaces of the garden in general. In very simplistic terms, any property has three principle divisions:

Front or **Public Space** — This part of the garden is for the owner's enjoyment as well as that of passersby.

Service Space — The driveway, garage, and storage areas are located here. The service space may also in-

clude utility gardens for fruits, vegetables, herbs, and cut flowers.

Private Space — This area can be an outdoor "living room" or pleasurable viewing area, but, as a use area, it should include a paved area for tables, chairs, and socializing; and a comfortable circulation (walkway) system for getting to and from other parts of the property.

With these space divisions in mind, define the specific use areas of the garden. Bubble diagrams are used to note the three or four space divisions and the specific use areas.

BUBBLE DIAGRAM OF USE AREAS

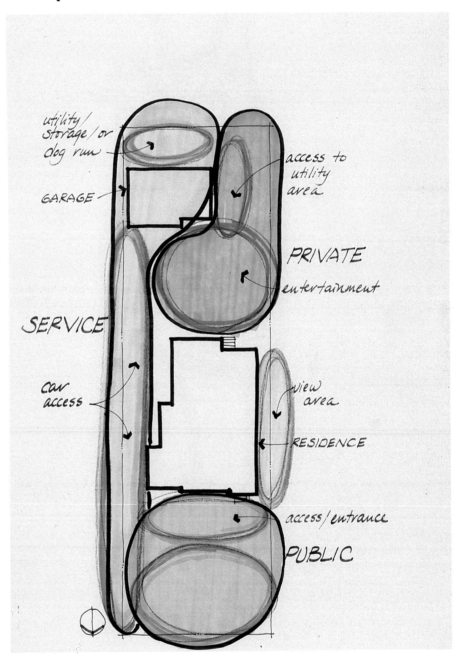

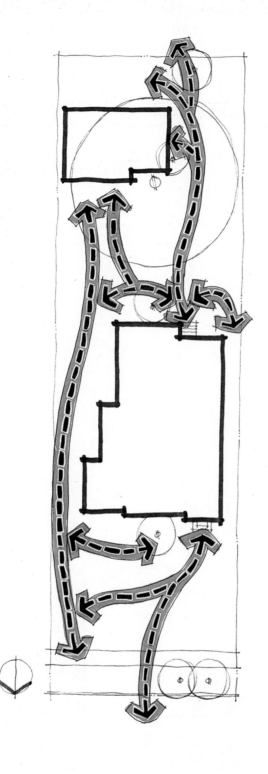

CIRCULATION STUDY

All you are studying in this first diagram is how different parts of your property relate to each other. In the Cole project on the preceding page, you can see that the use areas include: entrance, utility and storage, car access, and entertainment.

2. DEFINING CIRCULATION ROUTES

Next, use lines or arrows to connect those spaces. This will create the conceptual design for the circulation paths (walks, terraces, etc.).

In a small landscape such as the Coles', these circulation paths are limited to those shown at left. For larger, more complex sites, several alternative circulation routes can and should be considered.

3. REFINING THE CIRCULATION SYSTEM

The paving system can then be roughed in to coincide with the circulation pattern. Here, you will be drawing the route of the circulation system and the actual shape and dimensions of the pathways.

In the Cole project, the terrace was made as large as possible to accommodate frequent, small gatherings and occasional large parties. A swimming pool was considered, but found to be impractical for the space.

Alternative Front Walks and Planting

During conceptual design, it is always best to consider various alternatives. Designers who develop only *one* idea are limiting themselves and the creativity of the project.

As shown in the following sketches, any area can have a multitude of successful schemes. The key is to let materialize the one that's best for the situation and the owner.

These sketches show how the Coles' front garden area had a multitude of possible design solutions.

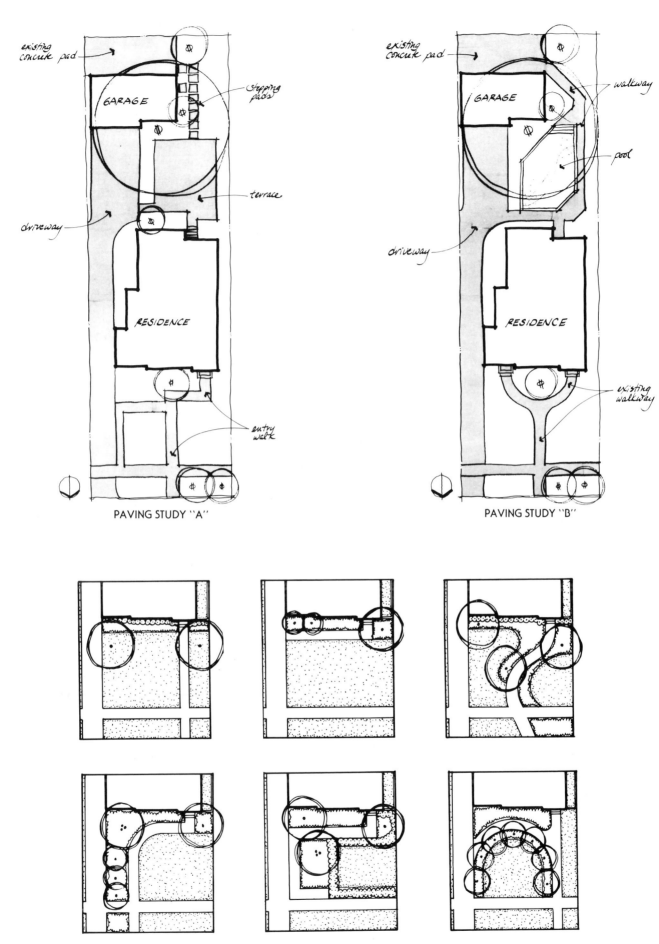

existing concrete pad

GARAGE

stepping pads

terrace

driveway

RESIDENCE

entry walk

PAVING STUDY "A"

existing concrete pad

GARAGE

walkway

pool

driveway

RESIDENCE

existing walkway

PAVING STUDY "B"

ALTERNATIVE FRONT WALKS AND PLANTING

4. ESTABLISHING MAJOR TREE LOCATIONS

With the paving concepts established in general, the rough tree-planting scheme can be laid out.

Although limited space prevents this sometimes, the ideal tree-planting concept is to use deciduous trees on the south and west sides for shade in summer and sun in winter. Evergreen plants should be planted on the north and east sides to block winter winds.

Trees introduced in the Cole project include new shade trees in front and back, ornamental trees for color in front and back, and fast-growing ornamental trees along the west property line to screen the view of neighboring houses. One upright tree was needed to shade the air conditioners and soften the east side of the house.

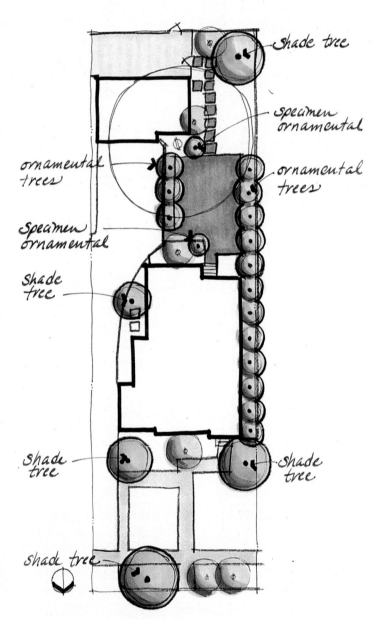

MAJOR TREE PLAN

14

5. DRAWING THE FINAL CONCEPTUAL PLAN

The drawing at this stage is still conceptual, but finalizes the overall look of the landscape. Trees, paving systems, and plant masses are shown; specific plants are not named at this point.

Although the five-step process is correct, in real life, when I design a project, I simply think through the first four steps and look at several conceptual-design alternatives. As a layman or beginning designer, even if you have to go back through the five steps each time, more than one conceptual design solution is essential.

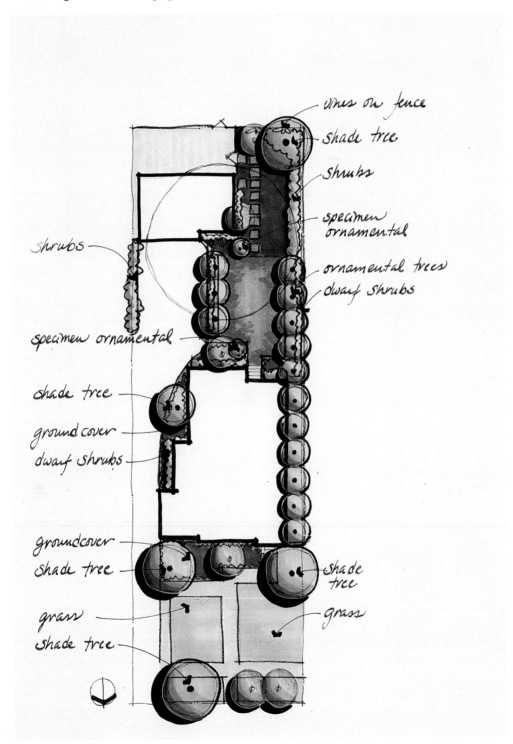

vines on fence
shade tree
shrubs
specimen ornamental
ornamental trees
dwarf shrubs
shade tree
grass
shrubs
specimen ornamental
shade tree
ground cover
dwarf shrubs
groundcover
shade tree
grass
shade tree

FINAL CONCEPTUAL PLAN

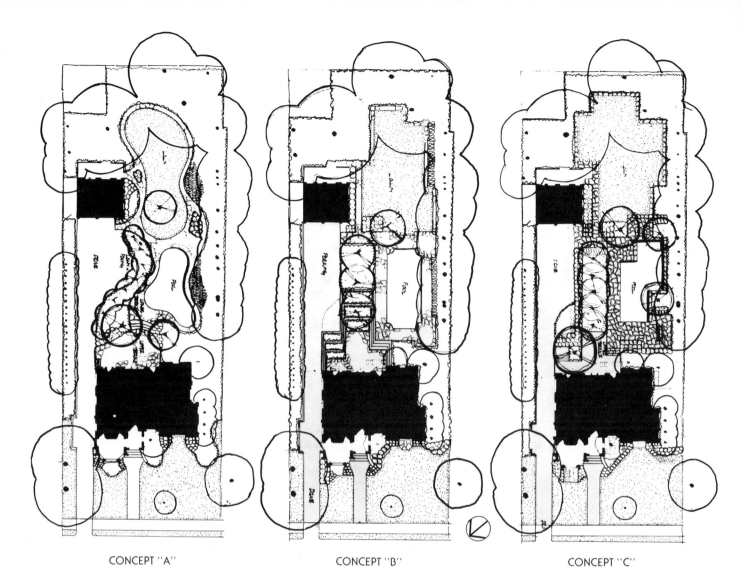

CONCEPT "A"   CONCEPT "B"   CONCEPT "C"

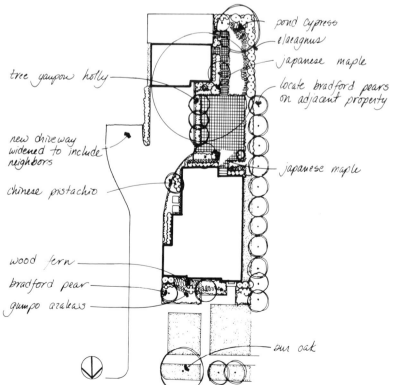

pond cypress
elaeagnus
japanese maple
locate bradford pears
on adjacent property

tree yaupon holly

new driveway
widened to include
neighbors

chinese pistachio

japanese maple

wood fern
bradford pear
gumpo azaleas

our oak

DESIGN DEVELOPMENT PLAN

Above are alternatives of another project, showing that any given space can have a multitude of successful design solutions. The secret to design is to allow the very best scheme to emerge.

Concept "A" shows a soft, curvilinear design while concepts "B" and "C" show crisp, straight-line design.

Design Development

Design development is the process of converting the conceptual design into a more detailed plan by naming materials and making the drawing accurate enough to prove that the scheme works. In simple projects, this step can be skipped and construction documents can be created directly from the concepts. This would apply to projects involving primarily plant material, with a limited amount of hard construction.

Construction Documents

Construction documents are drawings and written specifications used to build the project. They become part of the contract documents signed between the owner and landscape contractor. They consist of a demolition plan, layout/grading plan, lighting plan, construction details, irrigation plan, planting plan, and specifications.

Construction documents should be thorough enough to help the contractor understand completely how to build the project and, at the same time, provide the owner with the comfort that all foreseeable costs are covered. Although no set of plans or specs is perfect, some are much better than others.

It is important to spend money wisely on items that are not visible when the job is complete. The final documents should carefully identify the proper bed preparation and underground drainage for plants to be healthy and grow.

Attractive construction documents are worthless if they don't clearly and easily communicate to the contractor how to build the project.

Conversely, plain, simple, unartistic drawings that do explain the project to the contractor are very valuable to everyone involved. An ambitious homeowner may create these plans, but this step is more commonly undertaken by landscape architects.

Construction documents consist of the following:

DEMOLITION PLAN

This drawing depicts what will be torn out, and what areas are to be protected.

For the Cole project, we needed to remove the front and back sidewalks and the existing driveway. We had to protect the existing pecan and redbuds from construction damage.

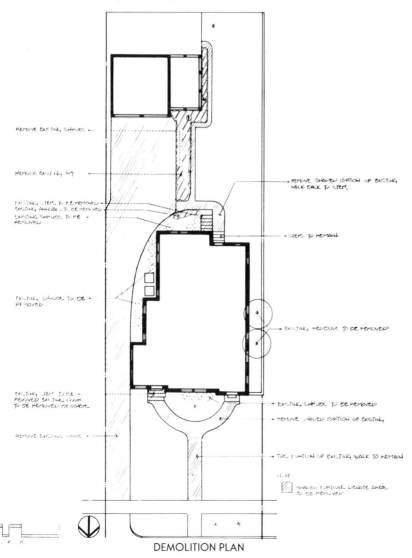

DEMOLITION PLAN

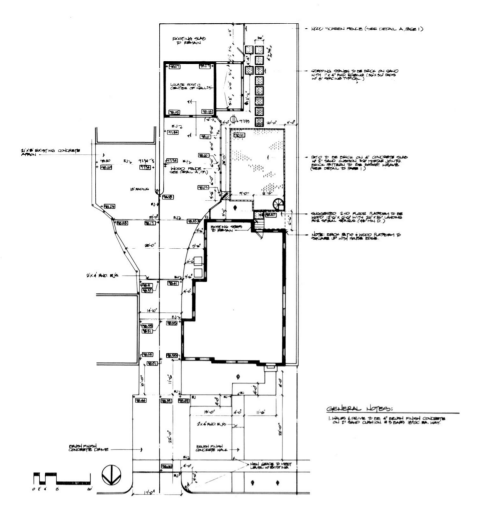

LAYOUT AND GRADING PLAN

This drawing shows accurately, by dimensions and grades, where the hard-construction elements are to be placed and how they will be installed.

Hard-construction elements installed at the Cole site were: new driveway, sidewalks, terrace, stepping stones, sprinkler system, garden room (conversion of maid's quarters), and fence between driveway and rear garden.

CONSTRUCTION DETAILS

The construction details are dimensional drawings that relate how to build the construction elements of the design.

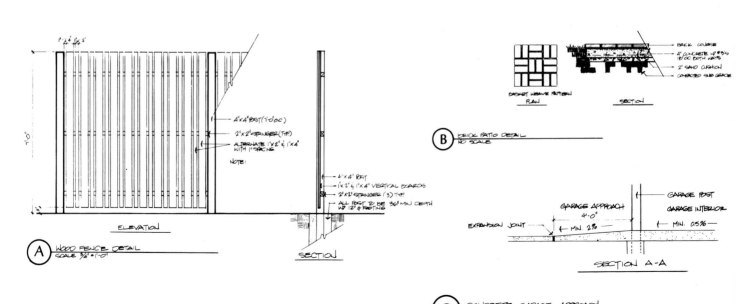

LIGHTING PLAN

The lighting plan shows the location of the Coles' light fixtures, their relative light levels, and the direction of light focus. Using a dark, black-line print and white pencil is a good way to illustrate the lighting scheme.

IRRIGATION PLAN

The Cole irrigation plan shows the sprinkler-head layout and specifies the size of pipe, kind of sprinkler heads, and the kind of valves and controllers that regulate the dispersion of the water through the irrigation system.

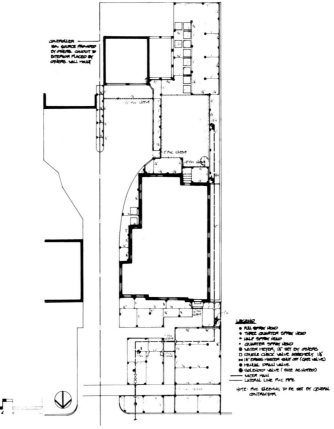

PLANTING PLAN

The planting plan shows the type, location, size, and spacing of each plant in the Cole plan. When a plan has a limited amount of hard con- struction, these structural elements, such as steel edging, small water features, and fences, will be shown on the planting plan.

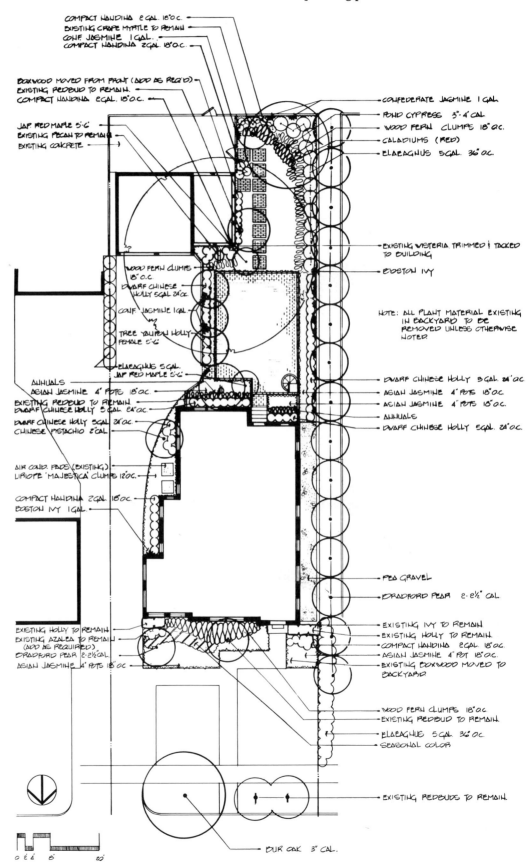

Specifications

Specifications are a set of typed documents accompanying the drawings that explain, in careful detail, how to build the project. While the construction-document drawings indicate the *quantity* of each element of the project, the written specifications outline the *quality* of each element. Specification categories are: demolition, site utilities, grading, sub-surface drainage, irrigation, planting and plant materials, hard construction, lighting, pools and spas, and maintenance.

Construction Administration

A design is successful only if the project is built properly. Designers, contractors, and owners need to work closely together to ensure the best possible execution of the landscape plan.

Good plans and specs are worthless if the owner or contractor doesn't install the work accordingly. A good landscape plan can become an unsuccessful landscape if, in the process, a tree is omitted, the pool is moved slightly, the exposed aggregate deck is changed to coolcrete, the fence is sloped instead of level, the pool plaster is white instead of gray green, and Indian hawthorn and azaleas are replaced by euonymus and boxwood.

So, be sure you follow the plans and specs! Modifications to the plan can be made, but should be included only after careful discussion by all parties concerned.

As-Built Plans

As-built plans are drawings of what was actually built, showing any alterations to the construction documents. They are primarily used to show underground elements such as utility lines, valves, etc., that were installed in a slightly different location than the original drawings. These changes are quite common during construction due to unpredictable circumstances.

Phasing the Cole Project

The Coles elected to install their project over a period of years, with the first year phase being the largest. It included the demolition of the old paving system and the construction of a new front walk, drive, and base concrete for the rear terrace.

The shade trees were planted in Phase 1, although small sizes were used, and the irrigation system was installed. Some ornamental trees and shrubs were installed and the remainder of the beds were filled with temporary annuals planted from seed.

Phase 2 included converting the maid's quarters into the garden room and building the new fences. Vines were planted on the fences at this time.

Phase 3 consisted of adding the brick paving to the concrete base of the terrace and stepping stones and installing the lighting system.

Phase 4 completed the shrub and ground cover planting.

The Cole Landscape Completed

Now that we've taken the Cole landscape through the step-by-step design process, let's review what we started with and look at the finished product.

The Cole landscape presented several design challenges: the site itself — a long, narrow lot; the need for entertainment space; and the owners' desire for low maintenance.

Specifically, there was no easy way to park in the driveway, and access to the front door was inconvenient. Many alternatives were considered; the following was chosen as the best landscape solution for the Cole family.

In the front, the driveway was widened into a common access for the Coles and their next-door neighbors; the drive was also tied into the walk system to provide a more comfortable access to the front door. A large, existing, purple redbud tree was saved, which helps frame the door and create an inviting feel for the entrance walk.

A large existing pecan tree was protected in the rear garden during the hard-construction phase. During this time, the walls were removed from the maid's quarters to create a garden room. The terrace and stepping-stones were then installed to connect the garden room and utility area.

(Left, top) The front door area.

(Left, bottom) The front walkway was constructed of lightly brushed, plain concrete, a clean-lined, economical choice.

(Right) The brick terrace, laid in a basketweave pattern, makes a pleasant contrast to the ophiopogon, wood fern, compact nandina, and annuals. Newly converted garden room is visible to the left.

(Top) A view from the rear garden area toward the house.

(Left) Brick stepping stones off the edge of the terrace.

(Right) The rear garden is lighted by mercury vapor downlights mounted in the large pecan tree.

(Left) The rough cedar fence, painted to match the color on the house, separates the rear garden from the driveway but allows light and air circulation. The materials used are 4x4-inch posts, 2x4-inch stringers, and 1x4-inch and 1x2-inch alternating boards.

(Right) A single mercury vapor ground light located correctly can light a large area for aesthetics and security.

III. *Installing Your Landscape*

ow that you've followed the Cole landscape design from start to finish, and you have an idea of how to design your own, how do we get your project built? Whether it is a do-it-yourself or professional job, the process is the same.

A major consideration here is the overall budget and how much of the budget is available for the first phase. Obviously, if money is available, installing the entire project at once is best. If the budget dictates that the project be phased, the most logical breakdown of the phasing process is to build all hard construction items first, but remember to leave access for those elements, such as swimming pools, if they are to be built later. Plant the shade trees next so they can begin their growth.

At this point I often recommend that more grass is planted than is to be ultimately used. While the trees are growing, the future ground cover and shrub beds can be temporarily grass. This is usually the time to install the irrigation system. The shrubs and ground covers can be planted later

when the trees begin to cast too much shade for grass to stay healthy. Some of my favorite projects are those where the landscape consists almost entirely of grass on gently rolling ground with deciduous trees. Provided access has been allowed for, the expensive recreational amenities, such as swimming pools and tennis courts, can be built as the last phases.

There are so many variables related to phasing it is difficult to recommend a cut-and-dried formula. The only sequencing issue I feel strongly about is that the shade trees should be planted in the early phases of any project.

It is important to think in terms of how long you will stay in the house. My recommended approach is somewhat different for those people planning to stay in a house 10 to 20 years, versus those planning to move on in 2 to 3 years.

Trees are the biggest variable here. If you plan to stay awhile, plant small trees (1- to 3-inch caliper) and let them grow. If it's to be a short stay, plant larger trees (3-inch caliper and up). Those of 5- to 6-inch caliper make the best initial impact. Resale value is what we're addressing here. There's no question in my mind that trees are by far the best investment in the landscape design. If the property has existing trees, that's even better; the first phase budget can be spent on other design elements.

When most people think of landscaping, they are thinking about plants. But in most cases, the landscape design is controlled more by the arrangement of buildings and hard construction than by the plants. Often, the house, terrace, driveways, and walks are in place when the owner buys the house. This is unfortunate since the builder usually installs these elements the same easy way each time, without any understanding or concern for the creation of the future garden spaces.

In the following pages, I'll address the hard-construction elements first because they are installed first, if you're lucky enough to be starting from scratch. However, if these hard-construction elements are already in your landscape, you may move on to the planting section of the book.

Hard Construction

In general terms, here's what I recommend:

Houses and other structures should be set at grades so their grade beams show as little as possible. I think the use of foundation planting became a common practice when houses began to be built with high, ugly concrete grade beams. With a little care, the grading and finished floor of the structures can be set where no grade beam shows and the drainage still works. (If you're forced to use foundation plantings, the best and most design-sensitive types include dwarf shrubs; ground covers; and, in some cases, grass.)

Even though the location and shapes of the drive, walks, and terraces have been selected by this point in the planning process, a tremendous range of cost is determined by what materials are chosen.

Plain gray brushed concrete is the most economical. Moving up the dollar scale, we find: exposed aggregate, treated pine decks, brick, stone, and, finally, redwood decks. Plain brushed concrete is usually the most practical for driveways and parking areas. Terraces and garden walks are most efficient when made of exposed aggregate concrete. If the budget allows, brick or stone is better. For grade change areas and spaces around existing trees, wood decks are best.

In phasing the hard-construction items, the driveway, walks to the house, and terraces have to be done in the beginning. On the walks and terraces, sometimes the base concrete can be done during Phase 1, used for awhile in that condition, and then brick or stone added later when money is available. (This is not a great idea because the brick or stone usually never gets installed.)

Fences and walls should go in next, completing the hard-construction part of the project. During the hard-construction phase, PVC (polyvinylchloride plastic) sleeves should be installed under all paving for future water, electrical, and sprinkler systems.

Pools are the most expensive single element of the garden design. Ideally, they should be built during the construction of the other hardscape elements. They can be phased in later, but great care must be taken to ensure access to build the pool, protection of established parts of the garden, and drainage from the pool.

The addition of tennis courts, bowling greens, greenhouses, putting greens, ponds, etc., needs the same considerations.

Working Around Existing Trees

All trees are important in one way or another. Some trees provide welcome shade, some bear fruit, all discourage erosion, clean the air, and produce oxygen. It is very important to be as sensitive as possible to these existing trees when working around them.

Mesquite, post oak, bur oak, and red oak are the toughest to work around. It is most important to leave mesquite and post oak as you find them. Their root systems are extreme-

Brick used on a concrete base adds color.

Steel edging should be installed ½ inch higher than the grade.

Concrete edging provides a wider edge for ease of maintenance. Wheels of equipment can ride on the hard surface.

ly sensitive to change. Keep construction and *all* traffic away from their root systems, and don't ever add irrigation to mesquite and post oaks.

Bur oak and red oak are the most sensitive to "wet feet," or water standing underground. Maintaining good, positive drainage is extremely important. (See drawings on page 39.)

Live oak and cedar elm are usually the easiest to work around, although that's not always a sure thing. All trees prefer their roots to remain undisturbed.

If existing trees are to be retained in a project, and in most cases they should be, the first and most important task of the designer is to protect and save the trees. Protection from stored construction materials, grade adjustments, and traffic is as important as protection against physical damage to limbs and trunks.

Here are some examples of protective devices:

Strap boards (never nail them) to the trunk of each tree to protect it from being hit and damaged by construction equipment.

A chain-link fence is an easy, economical way to protect a tree during construction. The fence should be installed as far away from the tree trunk as possible — ideally, at the drip line (foliage edge) — to keep traffic away from the root system. Snow fences or other fencing systems can also be used.

A third protective device, usually used in commercial installations, is

the "erosion fence," hay bales set uphill from trees to protect them from excessive water running down the slope. Water washing freely across a tree's root system can cause damage by either washing soil away from the roots or depositing soil on the roots.

It's always a fight to keep contractors and the owners away from the trees' root zones because it's usually inconvenient for them not to use the space around the trees. But that's tough. Trees are more important than the contractor's convenience. (Substantial monetary penalties will usually get their attention.) Building architects and owners could also do a much better job of enforcing protection of existing trees.

Edgings

To separate grass from other plants in the garden, bands of paving (concrete, brick, or stone) are used. These bands vary in width from 6 inches to walkway-size widths. This form of edging is more expensive than other materials, but provides much easier maintenance, since the wheels of mowers and edgers can roll on the mowing strip. This lowers maintenance costs and provides a more permanent edge that holds the shapes of the garden design in place through the years.

Steel — at least ⅛-inch thick — is the only other quality edging I would recommend. The advantage of steel over paved mowing strips is cost; steel

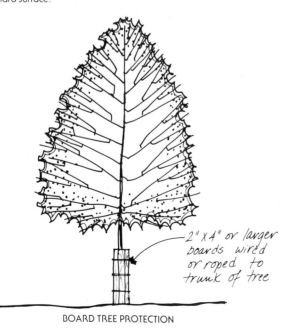

2" × 4" or larger boards wired or roped to trunk of tree

BOARD TREE PROTECTION

chain link fencing at drip line of tree

FENCE TREE PROTECTION

also tends to be less visible, which is helpful in some gardens.

There are several materials on the market that I would not recommend as edgings because they look bad and don't last. These include — but are not limited to — rubber, tin, wood, aluminum, and plastic. Using loose bricks or stones is also a bad idea because they shift, and because unwanted grass grows readily between the loose stones.

Terraces

The term "terrace" is a better word for what many people call "the patio." A patio is a small blob of hard surfacing, usually found at the back door. The terrace is an outdoor extension of the living space of the house. It is also the beginning of the outdoor circulation system, in that it is the heart or hub of the walk and path systems. In fact, sometimes the terrace *is* the path system.

The average amount of terracing in most gardens is too small, making circulation and entertainment areas too cramped. I guess people are worried about a sea of concrete, but that fear

Brick used on a concrete base adds color.

Stone used as an edging can be wider and serve as a walkway.

Concrete may be given a smooth or exposed finish.

Sandblasted concrete has a uniform texture and softer look.

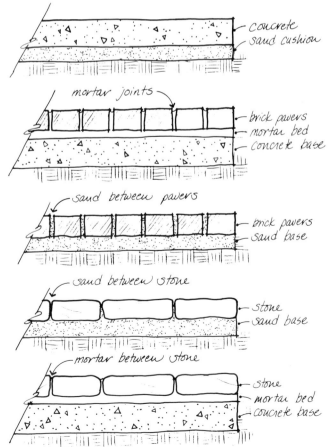

Cast stone combines well with exposed aggregate and brass skimmer cover.

Stone can be dressed to form a uniform edge.

TERRACE PAVING DETAILS

can be eliminated with the use of interesting patterns, materials, plants, and furniture. More terracing in the garden not only helps the circulation and function, but it also reduces maintenance.

Paths and Walkways

Paths may be made of many materials, from inexpensive bark or gravel surfaces to elaborate cut stone. They all serve basically the same purpose — providing a walking surface for touring the garden for maintenance and enjoyment. Paths also can function as mowing-strip edgings and as dividers of different plantings.

Paths for maintenance only can be as narrow as 18 inches; those for casual touring should be wider, ideally a minimum of 5 feet so two people can walk side by side.

Exposed aggregate, brick, and stone stepping stones.

Stone on sand makes a pleasant, informal paving surface.

Pea gravel under stone is also good; and, when extended past the stones, it becomes a design element.

Granite chips with steel or other edgings make a pleasant paving surface.

Formal brick walkway to front entrance.

Brick driveway turnaround.

Interlocking concrete-paver driveway.

Basketweave brick pattern.

Asphalt drive with brick edge.

When stone is used on pool decks, it can extend to become the coping.

30

Steps

Steps should be simple in design, and provide one of three functions: handle a grade change, mark an entry point, or separate one use area from another.

Grade Change — Steps may allow areas of different levels to flow together better than walls, although they serve the function of a retaining wall. Steps should be wide enough to be comfortable for their intended use, and the riser/tread relationship should be correctly proportioned. The illustration shows two comfortable riser/tread relationships. In general: the shorter the riser, the longer the tread. Allow a ⅛- to ¼-inch downward slope in the tread for drainage (include this figure in the overall riser height).

Marking a Point of Entry — Steps should signal an inviting point of entry to the circulation system. They can be important design features of the garden, but should not be too busy-looking; too many different materials and shapes will create a distraction from the rest of the garden.

Separating Areas — Steps can effectively define and separate one use area from another. For example, some gardens have upper areas that are more active and lower areas that are passive. Sometimes a pool is separated from the rest of the terrace by the use of steps.

Plain concrete steps.

Redwood walkway to front entrance.

Stone paving, when used with boulders, creates a natural edge. Note that the risers are a full stone in thickness.

Exposed aggregate (pea gravel) steps.

Curved Pennsylvania greenstone steps.

Steps can be as simple as plain concrete or wood.

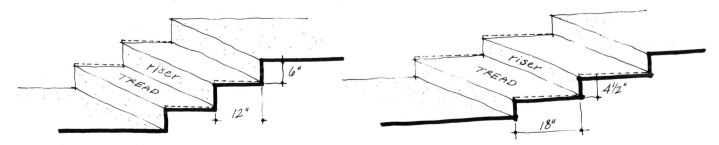

RISER-TREAD RELATIONSHIP

31

Decorative screen of 4x4 posts (7 feet o.c.), 2x4 stringers, and alternating 1x2's and 1x4's with 1-inch spaces between.

Decorative screen of 4x4 posts (7 feet o.c.), six 2x2 stringers, with alternating flat and on-end 1x2's.

Walls and Fences

Fences and walls do three things: retain soil, create privacy, and keep people and/or animals in or out of the landscape.

Retaining walls keep the soil and/or structures from moving, falling, sliding, and sloughing. All fences and walls are vertical elements, but retaining walls serve as much more than just a privacy and visual device. Retaining walls, being structural elements, should be designed and built very carefully because they are expensive *and* can be very dangerous when they fail.

Screening fences are used to create privacy by blocking views. Plants can also be used for this purpose, but solid fences and walls are more permanent and give instant screening. These fences need to be architecturally fitting and pleasing to look at on their own, or enhanced by plant materials.

Security fences are used to keep the kids and the pets in the yard, and the trespassers out. These fences are sometimes totally utilitarian, but, more often, also serve as important aesthetic design elements of the garden.

Overhead Structures

Arbors, pergolas, and trellises are all names for overhead structures. Why the different names, I don't know. They have three functions. They provide structures for vines to grow on, allowing very fast vertical greenery. They provide shade for the garden. They serve as focal points or terminators to a view in the garden.

Overhead structures are most commonly made of wood, but can also be made of steel, tension wire, brick, stone, or other materials.

Wood fence of 1x2 boards.

Unpainted chain-link.

Painted chain-link.

Wood dog-run fence. The dog can see out; people can't see in. Steel posts, alternating 2x2's and 1x8's, with 1-inch gap between boards.

Black dog-run fence and plain concrete paving.

Black chain-link fence with white brick columns.

Antique brick screening walls with Boston ivy.

Grape stake — great material, but hard to find.

Board-and-batten fence, decorative columns, and column cap.

Brick courtyard walls with decorative iron panels.

Painted brick wall with fig ivy.

Contemporary brick wall and iron gate.

Tennis court fence of tubular steel and welded wire mesh.

Wrought-iron security fence.

Chopped limestone wall with dark grout.

Simple wrought-iron fence and gate connected to a board-and-batten fence.

Dry limestone retaining wall sloped back for strength.

Mortared wall with deep joints gives the illusion of a dry-laid wall.

Irregular limestone wall with medium-gray grout.

Overhead structures can be very open and still create the feeling of enclosure. Even the Alamo has an overhead structure.

Rough-cut cedar is a good overhead structure material.

Overhead structures don't have to be flat.

Irrigation

Although the state's water supply is becoming more critical each year, irrigation systems are a must in all Texas cities. Spray systems are usually needed, since underground drip systems don't suffice for landscape irrigation, especially in clay soil. Even in sandy soil, the roots of plants grow solid around the pipe, preventing the water from spreading out evenly. To remedy this problem, more people are using systems that drip or bubble just above the surface at the base of each plant. The state of the art in irrigation does seem to be improving.

Underground drip systems do appear to work in vegetable and annual gardens, where the plants are changed seasonally. Here, the soil is very loose and friable, allowing the water to move laterally.

Quality systems consist of automatic time clocks, underground PVC pipe, copper stationary risers, brass spray heads, plastic high-pop heads, and large brass or plastic rotaries. Plastic stationary risers, which are unsightly and cheap-looking, are being used too often.

Without a doubt, water conservation will be of increasing importance to landscape design in the future. The ultimate solution, however, is not worldwide desert landscaping. A better idea is to design soft, green gardens — filled with plants that have reasonable water requirements — and install highly efficient irrigation systems.

Rotary heads are used in large areas.

Pop-ups are spray heads commonly used for grass areas.

High pop heads are used in ground cover and shrub beds near heavy traffic.

Bubblers are used for flood irrigating, contained planting beds, or individual trees.

Stationary risers are used in shrub and ground-cover beds. Materials should be copper risers and brass heads.

Xeriscape

There's a lot of talk about Xeriscape these days. Xeriscape is a new buzzword meaning practical landscaping that requires a minimum amount of irrigation.

I agree with most of the concepts that are being preached about Xeriscape, such as:

- Add plenty of organic material to shrub and ground-cover beds to hold in moisture.
- Use native plants, such as cedar elm, red oak, redbud, and sumac.
- Mow lawn grasses slightly higher than normal, to about 3 inches.
- Mulch planting beds to keep beds cool, moist, and weed-free.
- Provide thorough, regular fertilization and insect/disease control for all plant materials. Also, check irrigation systems regularly.
- Use an above-ground drip system where practical, since less water is lost to evaporation with this system.
- Avoid using inefficient sprinklers that spray into streets and against buildings.
- To avoid fogging, use pressure-reducing valves.
- Use rainstats on sprinkler systems to avoid wasting water during and after rains.

However, I *don't* believe in:

- Underground drip systems for everything. They might work for flower and vegetable gardens in sandy soil.
- Inorganic mulches, such as plastic.
- The extensive use of gravel and desert plants.
- Using certain scraggly native plants, which are beautiful only a very short portion of the year.
- Using tiny spray heads, which become clogged with algae and salts.

Xeriscapers also tend to forget to mention that trees go a long way toward preserving soil moisture by shading the ground.

Drainage

Since much of the soil in Texas drains so poorly, it is amazing how long it has taken landscape architects and contractors here to understand how important positive drainage, not just surface drainage, is — particularly around trees.

We now use underground drainage on all projects where the chance of excessive soil moisture exists. If the project uses only umbrella plants, sweet gum, and bald cypress, underground drainage is not needed. Any other plants can benefit greatly from drainage pipe.

The most important feature of drainage is that the system takes away the water and prevents the soil from staying wet. It's also important, from a design standpoint, that the above-ground portions of the drainage system do not detract from the look of the overall landscape design.

A brass or cast-iron grate should be used instead of plastic. Plastic isn't durable or attractive.

Bee-hive grates are used in planting beds. They are resistant to becoming clogged with leaves.

Round, custom-made slot drain.

Swimming pool.

Water Features

Water is important to almost any garden. Many people are intimidated about the cost of water features, but not all of them are expensive. Some can be very simple and inexpensive. In fact, since the most important asset of water in the garden is the sound, simplicity is usually encouraged. However, if budget allows, large dramatic features should be considered and, in some garden spaces, are *needed*.

Water features fall into one of six different categories: flumes, geysers, walls, streams, ponds, and pools.

Flume.

Multi-geyser.

Single geyser.

Wall.

Stream.

Natural pond.

Structured pool.

Spa.

Tennis Courts

Tennis courts are for playing tennis — period. Each court is very large, requiring a minimum of 60x120 feet. It has to be built very carefully. Structural problems are a real concern, and no system is foolproof. It's always advisable to consult a structural engineer before installing a tennis court on your property. Besides being large, a tennis court has other problems that must be addressed in the design. A tennis court requires a fence about 10 feet high which can be ugly, and its lighting must be sensitive (unobtrusive) to the neighborhood.

Children's Play Areas

Children's play areas have gotten too commercial-looking in the past several years. In fact, we landscape architects are at fault for designing some of the heavy and expensive store-bought equipment that has been introduced to parks and residences.

The design of kids' play areas should be simple and have three basic elements: a hard surface — preferably a path — on which to ride trikes and pull wagons; a simple climbing apparatus or a tree; and a sandbox in which to play.

Since the children's area is a temporary need, the area should have the flexibility of being converted to some other function or permanent planting space when the kids have left home to terrorize other people.

Recessed tennis court uses concrete retaining wall and black iron with welded wire fence.

A tennis court tucked into the back portion of the property and buffered by a wee burn, bridge, and planting.

Wood posts with soft netting.

Brick wall with black/brown chain link hides the tennis court from view.

A climbing apparatus or tree is always needed.

Kids enjoy circling 'round.

Play surface of pea-gravel.

Planting

One of the biggest misconceptions is that landscape installation should be done in the spring. That's the worst time. Contractors and nurseries are busier in the spring and early summer than at any other time of the year.

Any landscape installation is best done in the fall and winter. If plants are installed in the fall, they will develop some root growth through the dormant season and be more vigorous in the spring.

Trees, especially, should be transplanted and/or planted in the fall or winter. Trees planted in the spring, and certainly in the summer, will just sit there and wait for the next season to really start to grow.

With fall and winter planting, there *is* some danger of freeze damage, mainly to small shrubs, ground covers, and grasses. You may prefer to install these small plants in the spring. The major elements (hard construction, trees, and large shrubs) are not usually susceptible to freeze damage.

Planting Trees

It is best to plant the shade trees first if phasing the project, and then plant the ornamental trees later.

Each tree hole should be at least 2 feet larger in diameter than its root ball. After the hole is dug, it's a good idea to fill the hole with water to see how well the soil drains. If the water

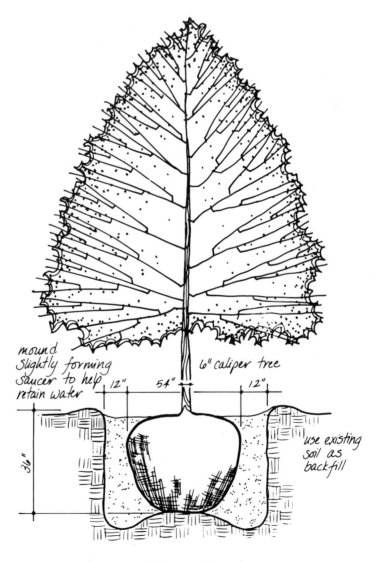

mound slightly forming saucer to help retain water

6" caliper tree

12"   54"   12"

36"

use existing soil as backfill

TREE PLANTING DETAIL

stays in the hole for more than a day, add one of two drainage solutions:

1. Pier hole (sump) — Dig down through the bottom of the tree hole until you reach rock or other soil-structure change. The pier, 4 to 10 inches in diameter, should be filled with coarse gravel. Pipe isn't necessary. This is the simpler, less costly solution.

2. Drainage lines — Run flexible or rigid perforated plastic pipe from the bottom of the tree hole sloping down to the storm sewer system, to daylight, or through the curb to the street. This pipe should be 4 inches in diameter or greater and should be surrounded by gravel. When this system isn't feasible, use the pier-hole solution.

Installing a PVC pipe vertically, beside the ball, is sometimes employed so that excess water can be pumped out. Often, this doesn't work well because people forget to pump out the water. In fact, it's a pretty stupid thing to do. We've done it in the past and about all you get is the pleasure of seeing an exposed white pipe end and cap.

Now you're ready to install your trees. When planting, make sure that the top of the root ball is flush with the ground surface.

The next step is to take off all wrapping from the trunk and remove ropes from the top of the root ball and from around the trunk. This is especially critical if the rope is synthetic. Since it won't rot, it can cut into the trunk and eventually kill the tree.

Next, backfill around the ball with existing soil taken from the hole. If the hole is solid rock, mix topsoil from a nearby area with some of the broken rock from the hole. Water-in the soil thoroughly, then tamp down the soil around the root ball. This helps hold the tree in place, eliminates the need for tree staking, and discourages air pockets.

A small mound of earth 3 to 6 inches high can be built around the outside edge of the hole to create a saucer effect to aid in thorough watering. This ring should be removed after the tree has been planted for one year. Since these rings aren't attractive, they can be eliminated from the start if you are very careful to soak the root ball every two weeks during the hot

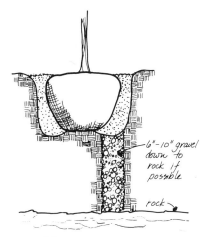

6"–10" gravel down to rock if possible

rock

GRAVEL SUMP TO ROCK

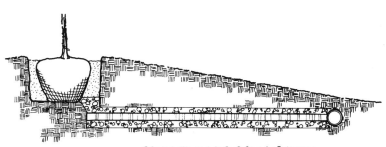

DRAIN TO MAJOR DRAIN SYSTEM

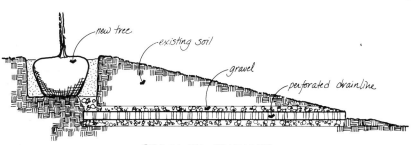

new tree

existing soil

gravel

perforated drainline

DRAIN TO DAYLIGHT

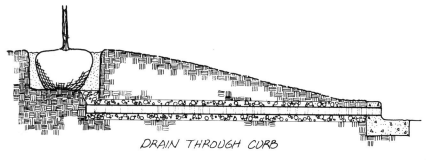

DRAIN THROUGH CURB

DRAINAGE DETAIL

An insect would have to be pretty stupid not to be able to figure out how to get through this to the tree.

weather. This deep soaking should be done in addition to the regular watering, but only should be done if the soil is draining well.

If someone suggests that improved soil (sand, organic matter, or any combination thereof) should be used instead of the native soil, tell them to go away. The root system will grow quickly into the native soil, so why start the roots in something different? Huge amounts of money are wasted on this improper procedure. With the rising cost of everything these days, it's foolish to waste money on unnecessary procedures.

STAKING TREES

The best way to "stake" a tree is not to do it at all. You won't need this procedure if the tree's ball is large enough to provide enough roots, which act as an anchor. All tree staking looks bad, is a maintenance problem, girdles the tree, restricts the tree from developing support roots, and slows growth.

If the proper root-ball size (of at least 9 inches of ball per caliper inch of trunk diameter) is used, and the backfilled soil is watered-in thoroughly and tamped securely, there is no need for staking or guying. Two exceptions: Palm trees and pine trees, because of their small root systems, usually have to be staked.

TREE WRAPPING

Wrapping cloth, tape, or other miscellaneous dressings around tree trunks is another waste of time and money. The covering restricts the natural toughening process of the bark, harbors insects and disease, and looks terrible.

Planting Shrubs, Ground Covers, and Vines

Unlike trees, these plants need some bed preparation. Since their root systems are small and remain in the prepared area until the plants mature, it's wise to add sand and organic matter to clay soils, and organic material and lime to sandy acid soils.

To prepare a shrub bed, allow for and add 3 inches of organic material to the bed. Then add a light applica-

tion of fertilizer and rototill to a depth of 8 inches to thoroughly mix all additives with the existing soil.

When preparing a ground cover bed, allow for and add 2 inches of organic material to the bed. Then add a light application of fertilizer and rototill to a depth of 4 inches to thoroughly incorporate additives into the existing soil.

In any soil, it is very important for moisture to exist in the soil prior to planting. Although planting in the hot months is not our recommendation, sometimes it is essential. **Moisten the dry soil prior to planting.** This is very important for shrubs and ground cover plants. The hot, dry soil can suck the moisture from the plant's root system before you have time to water in the new planting.

Key to plant establishment is consistent watering and regular light cultivation of the bare soil around the plants. This process eliminates compaction, opens the soil for air and water, and weeds the beds at the same time. Cultivation can be substantially eliminated by mulching the bare areas around the plants.

Planting Annuals and Perennials

Flowers need even better bed preparation than shrubs, because you want the plants to grow and flower quickly. Also, you'll need to be making changes during the growing season. Planting new annuals and perennials in soft, loose soil is very pleasant. Digging around in clay and rock is *not*. Having moist soil prior to planting is, again, very important.

To prepare an annual or perennial bed, follow the direction above for shrub-bed preparation, with the following addition: supplemental sharp sand and organic material. Flower beds need to be very deeply prepared and friable. For best results, add a minimum of 6 inches of sand and 3 inches of organic material, or, better still, 50 percent sand and 50 percent organic material.

My recommendation for planting flowers is to plant what pleases you. I tend to like large masses of like plants to make a dramatic impact, although small, surprising splashes of color in the garden can be very pleasant. Since I am always experimenting in my garden, mine has a little of everything in most parts. But do as I say, not as I do!

Planting Grass

Unless the ground is solid rock, improving the soil prior to planting grass is a waste of time and money. As long as the soil isn't hard compacted, most grasses can be planted in all forms right on the existing soil. If the soil is hard compacted, loosen by plowing or rototilling. The seed bed should then be raked smooth before planting the grass. Make sure no low spots or large flat areas remain that will hold water. Poor drainage is a killer for most plants.

The cheapest and easiest way to plant grass yourself is to sow the seed by hand, and water evenly until establishment. It's better — and even easier — to hire a grass company to blow the seed on the ground by a process known as hydromulching. Cool-season grasses (fescue, blue, rye) should be planted in the fall (September 15th at the earliest); Bermuda grasses should be planted between June 1st and August 31st. Solid sod may be planted anytime, although there is some danger of freeze when planted in the fall or winter in the colder parts of the state.

St. Augustine and zoysia should always be planted as solid sod. These grasses, especially zoysia, spread too slowly to be planted as plugs or sprigs. The key to the successful establishment of new grasses is to keep them evenly moist until the roots have grown in.

Transplanting Plants

In general, plants, especially trees, should be moved during the dormant seasons (fall and winter). Plants can be moved when they are growing, but the percentage of loss is much greater.

When lifting a tree, use chain or strap harnesses around the ball; *never* lift a tree by its trunk. This not only can damage the bark and underlying life-supporting layer, it also can loosen the roots from the root ball. (Remember, the proper root-ball size is at least 9 inches of ball per inch of trunk diameter.)

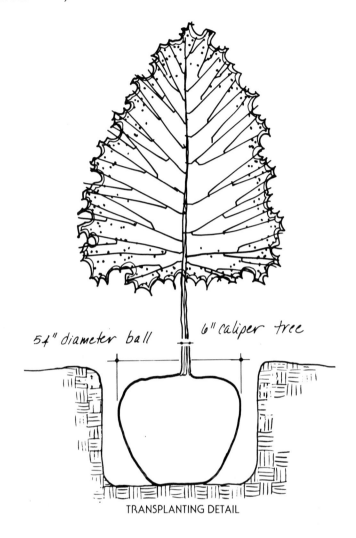

54" diameter ball   6" caliper tree

TRANSPLANTING DETAIL

Plant Materials

*T*his section explains and illustrates how plants are used as tools in garden design. They are very important, especially to the ultimate character and feel of the space. Rather than cover all the plant materials that work in Texas, presented are, in our opinion, the best and most foolproof for each plant zone area of Texas.

With our continuing hunger to learn more and more about new techniques, procedures, and plants, our best recommendations vary and have to be flexible. For example, here's a list of the casualties of the 1983 freeze: Indian hawthorn, wax ligustrum, Japanese ligustrum, live oak, crape myrtle, dwarf nandina 'nana,' and pittosporum. We used to recommend these plants highly and, even though we still use them in certain parts of Texas and in certain conditions, we are more cautious now. We try to warn clients that damage may occur again.

On the other hand, we are using more and more of the toughest plants. (More on that in the following pages, which specify plants for your area.) Another local landscape architect once commented that we can't just stop using all the plants that might freeze or otherwise die; the garden would be too boring. That's a silly comment. It seems to me that having a small variety of good, healthy, *live* plants is much better than an interesting variety of dead ones.

Plant Hardiness Map

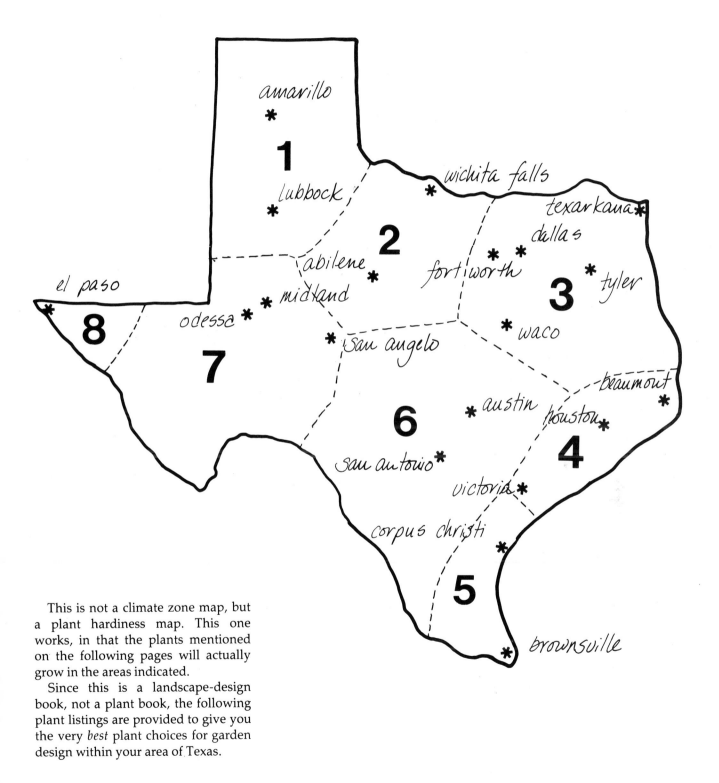

This is not a climate zone map, but a plant hardiness map. This one works, in that the plants mentioned on the following pages will actually grow in the areas indicated.

Since this is a landscape-design book, not a plant book, the following plant listings are provided to give you the very *best* plant choices for garden design within your area of Texas.

The Best Plants For Each Area In Texas

AREA 1

(Lubbock, Amarillo)

TREES	SHRUBS	GROUND COVERS & VINES	FLOWERS	GRASSES
Ash	Barberry	Virginia Creeper	Caladium	Bermuda
Crab Apple	Cotoneaster	Purple Euonymus	Chrysanthemum	Blue Grass
Cedar Elm	Elaeagnus	Honeysuckle	Copperleaf	Fescue
Chinese Elm	Dwarf Burford Holly	English Ivy	Lantana	
Honey Locust	Nellie R. Stevens Holly	Wilton Juniper	Marigold	
Pecan	Juniper	Liriope	Periwinkle	
Austrian Pine	Compact Nandina	Lady Banksia Rose	Verbena	
Pistachio		Silver-Lace Vine		
Purple Plum				
Redbud				
Red Oak				

Believe it or not, there are many good plants that will grow in Amarillo, but great care is needed in selection. Unfortunately, most of the oldest trees in the area are Siberian elms, and, being poor trees, they are slowly dying out, as they are all over the United States. It will take some time for the younger, more appropriate trees to mature and fill out.

Although I haven't seen any bur oaks growing in this area, I think that they should be introduced in limited quantities. The Chinese (Drake) elm does well, as does the cedar elm. The best tree by far is the red oak.

Places in the area to see interesting landscaping:

Lubbock: Texas Tech University, MacKenzie State Park, Buffalo Springs Lake

Amarillo: Amarillo College, downtown Amarillo

AREA 2

(Wichita Falls, Abilene)

TREES	SHRUBS	GROUND COVERS & VINES	FLOWERS	GRASSES
Crab Apple	Elaeagnus	Honeysuckle	Caladium	Common Bermuda
Cedar Elm	Indian Hawthorn	Boston Ivy	Chrysanthemum	Fescue
Yaupon Holly	Dwarf Burford Holly	English Ivy	Copperleaf	St. Augustine
Mesquite	Dwarf Chinese Holly	Asian Jasmine	Lantana	
Bur Oak	Nellie R. Stevens Holly	Carolina Jessamine	Marigold	
Red Oak	Juniper	Wilton Juniper	Periwinkle	
Bradford Pear	Compact Nandina	Liriope	Verbena	
Pecan	Photinia	Lady Banksia Rose		
Eldarica Pine		Trumpet Vine		
Pistachio		Virginia Creeper		
Redbud				

Bur oak and pistachio haven't been used very much in this area, but are thriving there in limited numbers. I would recommend using more of them. Many live oaks were killed in this area during the freeze of 1983, but even more died in the Dallas area. Plant live oaks at your own risk. There are more existing pecan trees growing here than any other variety of large tree. Someday there will be a magnificent stand of huge pecan trees all over the Wichita Falls/Abilene area.

Places in the area to see interesting landscaping:

Abilene: Downtown, Fairway Oaks, Buffalo Gap, Nelson Park Zoo

Wichita Falls: Midwestern State University

AREA 3

(Dallas, Fort Worth, Waco, East Texas)

TREES	SHRUBS	GROUND COVERS & VINES	FLOWERS	GRASSES
Cedar Elm	Elaeagnus	Boston Ivy	Caladium	Bermuda
Crape Myrtle	Dwarf Burford Holly	English Ivy	Chrysanthemum	St. Augustine
Yaupon Holly	Dwarf Chinese Holly	Gill Ivy	Copperleaf	Zoysia
Japanese Maple	Dwarf Yaupon Holly	Asian Jasmine	Lantana	
Bur Oak	Nellie R. Stevens Holly	Carolina Jessamine	Marigold	
Red Oak	Compact Nandina	Liriope	Periwinkle	
Bradford Pear	Photinia	Ophiopogon	Verbena	
Pecan	Sumac	Trumpet Vine		
Pistachio		Wisteria		
Redbud				

Azaleas, camellias, and dogwood trees also grow very well in this area, if the beds are sandy and acidic. I recommend azaleas be planted only in solid (100-percent) peat moss in *all* parts of Texas.

Bald cypress and sweet gum trees will grow anywhere in this area where rock is not found too near the soil surface. Some people know that the bald cypress likes plenty of water, but few know that sweet gum trees need at least as much or more water. Neither requires unusual amounts of water once established.

Places in the area to see interesting landscaping:

Dallas: Dallas Zoo, Dallas Arboretum and Botanical Garden, Old City Park, Dallas Civic Garden Center, Turtle Creek, Oak Cliff residential areas, Park Cities residential area

Arlington: Six Flags Over Texas

Fort Worth: Fort Worth Botanical Garden, Museum District

Waco: Baylor University

Tyler: Tyler Rose Gardens, Tyler Courthouse (on the lawn is an 80-foot-tall ginkgo, the largest in Texas)

Winnsboro: Autumn Trails Festival (annually in October)

AREA 4

(Houston, Victoria, Beaumont)

TREES	SHRUBS	GROUND COVERS & VINES	FLOWERS	GRASSES
Bald Cypress	Aralia	Boston Ivy	Caladium	Bermuda
Chinese Elm	Bottlebrush	English Ivy	Calendula	St. Augustine
Yaupon Holly	Indian Hawthorn	Fig Ivy	Chrysanthemum	Zoysia
Crape Myrtle	Dwarf Burford Holly	Confederate Jasmine	Copperleaf	
Bur Oak	Dwarf Chinese Holly	Asian Jasmine	Marigold	
Live Oak	Nellie R. Stevens Holly	Carolina Jessamine	Petunia	
Red Oak	Compact Nandina	Liriope	Verbena	
Water Oak	Photinia	Ophiopogon		
Bradford Pear	Pittosporum	Wisteria		
Pistachio	Viburnum			
Redbud				

The best thing about this area is that most anything will grow here. Just make sure to give all planting areas good positive drainage since the water table is high and rainfall is plentiful. If you live in this area, the pruning section of this book is particularly critical.

Places in the area to see interesting landscaping:

Houston: Rice University, Houston Arboretum, River Oaks, The Woodlands (north of the city on I-45)

Beaumont: The Big Thicket (north of the city)

AREA 5

(Corpus Christi, Brownsville)

TREES	SHRUBS	GROUND COVERS & VINES	FLOWERS	GRASSES
Ash	Aralia	Bougainvillea	Caladium	Bermuda
Yaupon Holly	Elaeagnus	Clematis	Calendula	St. Augustine
Crape Myrtle	Indian Hawthorn	English Ivy	Hibiscus	Zoysia
Live Oak	Dwarf Burford Holly	Fig Ivy	Lantana	
Fan Palm	Dwarf Yaupon Holly	Asian Jasmine	Petunia	
Washington Palm	Compact Nandina	Confederate Jasmine		
Bradford Pear	Oleander	Carolina Jessamine		
Pecan	Sago Palm	Liriope		
Japanese Black Pine	Variegated Pittosporum	Ophiopogon		
Mexican Plum	Natal Plum			

Palms are the trees you expect to see in this area; indeed, several varieties do very well here, including the fan and Washington palms. Many other varieties of tropical and semi-tropical plants thrive in this area.

Places in the area to see interesting landscaping:

Corpus Christi: Ocean Drive

Brownsville: Gladys Porter Zoo

AREA 6

(Austin, San Antonio)

TREES	SHRUBS	GROUND COVERS & VINES	FLOWERS	GRASSES
Ash	Bottlebrush	Honeysuckle	Caladium	Bermuda
Cedar Elm	Elaeagnus	Boston Ivy	Chrysanthemum	St. Augustine
Yaupon Holly	Indian Hawthorn	English Ivy	Copperleaf	Zoysia
Texas Mountain Laurel	Dwarf Burford Holly	Asian Jasmine	Daylily	
Bur Oak	Dwarf Yaupon Holly	Carolina Jessamine	Lantana	
Live Oak	Nellie R. Stevens Holly	Liriope	Marigold	
Red Oak	Compact Nandina	Ophiopogon	Periwinkle	
Bradford Pear	Photinia	Trumpet Vine	Plumbago	
Pecan	Pittosporum	Wisteria	Verbena	
Pistachio	Plumbago			
	Senecia			

Understanding how to plant in solid rock is the key to this area. Selecting the correct plant materials also is crucial. I hope the above list helps.

Places in the area to see interesting landscaping:

Austin: Zilker Park, Town Lake area, State Capitol

San Antonio: Sunken Gardens at Breckenridge State Park, The Alamo, The San Antonio Botanical Center, Riverwalk (downtown)

AREA 7

(Midland, Odessa, San Angelo)

TREES	SHRUBS	GROUND COVERS & VINES	FLOWERS	GRASSES
Ash	Barberry	Virginia Creeper	Caladium	Bermuda
Cedar Elm	Elaeagnus	Purple Euonymus	Chrysanthemum	Tall Fescue
Yaupon Holly	Dwarf Chinese Holly	Honeysuckle	Copperleaf	
Bur Oak	Dwarf Yaupon Holly	Boston Ivy	Lantana	
Red Oak	Nellie R. Stevens Holly	English Ivy	Marigold	
Pecan	Juniper	Wilton Juniper	Periwinkle	
Austrian Pine	Compact Nandina	Silver-Lace Vine	Verbena	
Eldarica Pine	Photinia	Trumpet Vine		
Pistachio	Senecia	Vinca Major		
Purple Plum		Wisteria		

This is a hard-to-grow area for plants. Selecting the toughest plants and using an efficient irrigation system is the key. Although normally I don't recommend euonymus, this is an area in which it does very well and is not plagued by the insect and disease problems common to other areas.

Places in the area to see interesting landscaping:

Midland: Rose Gardens (west of downtown), Residential areas

Odessa: Residential areas

San Angelo: Water lily garden at the Tom Green County Courthouse

AREA 8
(El Paso)

TREES	SHRUBS	GROUND COVERS & VINES	FLOWERS	GRASSES
Ash	Elaeagnus	Coyote Brush	Caladium	Bermuda
Mexican Elder	Fountain Grass	Honeysuckle	Chrysanthemum	Fescue
Yaupon Holly	Pampas Grass	English Ivy	Copperleaf	
Mesquite	Indian Hawthorn	Lady Banksia Rose	Daylily	
Russian Olive	Nellie R. Stevens Holly	Rosemary	Iris	
Pecan	Juniper		Lantana	
Eldarica Pine	Photinia		Marigold	
Pistachio	Senecia		Periwinkle	
Redbud	Yucca		Verbena	
Desert Willow				

This area is often ignored in landscaping books, so I hope this information helps the people who live in this beautiful part of Texas. I have seen one very healthy bur oak growing in El Paso, and I recommend that more are tried. As in the rest of the state, the pecan does well. (It was a great choice for the state tree!) I was introduced to an ash tree called 'Raywood' that I would recommend trying. It has a darker green color than most other ash trees and has a mahogany fall color. Mulberry trees have been used more than any other tree and that must *stop* — they're just as junky in El Paso as anywhere else! Other good plants to try in this dry climate are green sage, quail bush, creosote, desert broom, and artemesia.

Places in the area to see interesting landscaping:
University of Texas at El Paso (the architecture is great also!)
Upper Valley neighborhood
The natural scenery around the city

51

Trees

Trees are the most important design tool. The skillful use of all plant materials and hard-construction materials is important, but take away all the elements of a garden one by one, and the most-missed element will be the trees.

Nothing pleases people and creates an atmosphere quite like trees do. Other elements such as terraces and paths, smaller plant materials, lighting, etc., are important, but take existing trees away from any project and their absence is clearly felt. Trees invite us, shade us, surprise us, house wildlife, create backdrops and garden niches, and inspire and humble us.

Not only are trees the most important element from a design sensitivity standpoint, but they are also the most cost-effective design tool. For instance, what's more effective — $20,000 worth of sculpture, $20,000 worth of water, $20,000 worth of shrubs, or $20,000 worth of trees? The trees. Real-estate experts will tell you that a house surrounded by beautiful trees is worth much more than a house on a bare lot.

This certainly doesn't mean these other elements are not important or shouldn't be used. It simply means that if a budget is limited, concentrate on the trees first.

The trees shown in photos on the following pages are the very best for Texas. All trees have some value, but this information should help you prioritize the trees you might want to use.

It may be of interest to note that the trees most often used in landscape projects in Texas are: live oak, cedar elm, red oak, sweet gum, and crape myrtle. I'm not saying that's right, that's just how it is.

There's one thing I almost forgot to mention: using nothing but straight trees is boring. Crooked trees with interesting branching character are strong design elements and usually can be purchased for less money than perfectly straight, symmetrical trees.

ASH
Fraxinus texensis   Areas: All

Ash trees can be purchased in many varieties, all of which are fast-growing and relatively problem-free. They seem to be healthiest in the drier parts of the state. The Texas ash is a fast-growing native tree that has dark, deeply fissured bark, and the fall color ranges from yellow through orange and salmon to red. There are many beautiful specimens around Texas. This ash has an upright but symmetrical form, and larger leaflets than other ash trees.

CRAB APPLE
Malus Spp.   Areas: All

There are many beautiful varieties of crab apples; they probably should be used more. Their colorful spring blooms and fruit are pleasant garden additions. They will grow best in the cooler parts of the state.

CRAPE MYRTLE
Lagerstroemia indica   Areas: 2, 3, 4, 5, 6

This is Texas' most colorful ornamental tree with summer flowers of white, pink, red, and lavender. An often-overlooked attribute is its fall color. The fall color is red on the pink and lavender varieties, and yellow on the white varieties.

One problem with crape myrtles is that many people plant very small trees. After weed eaters get through whacking the bases and uninformed pruners whack the tops, there's nothing left. The bark is very tender, so weed eaters should not be used. The best pruning practice for crape myrtles is to leave them alone. Don't even cut off the seed pods — they're quite attractive. These trees may freeze, as they did during the '83-'84 winter.

BALD CYPRESS
Taxodium distichum   Areas: 2, 3, 4, 5, 6

Bald cypress grows naturally in lowlands around water, but it will adapt to urban settings. The lacy, upright tree looks somewhat like a pine, but is deciduous — with reddish brown fall color. It looks great used singularly or in masses.

Bald cypress has few insect or disease problems. It must be irrigated unless planted in a low, poorly drained area, but requires no more

Ash.

Ash.

Crab Apple.

Crab Apple.

Crape Myrtle.

Crape Myrtle.

Bald Cypress.

Crape Myrtle.

53

Bald Cypress.

water than most other trees.

Some lovely specimens and their overall effects can be seen at the Diamond Shamrock Tower in downtown Dallas; more are being planted in Dallas' Arts District. Of course, the most beautiful specimens are along the Riverwalk in downtown San Antonio. Note: Always specify and/or purchase by height instead of caliper.

POND CYPRESS
Taxodium ascendens   Areas: 2, 3, 4, 5, 6

This is a wonderful, but hard-to-find, tree. The pond cypress is a faster-growing version of the bald cypress. The best examples of these in Dallas are at 5401 Central at McCommas. There is also a fine specimen on Turtle Creek Boulevard, and another on the Lakewood Country Club Golf Course (both in Dallas). Although native to other states, the pond cypress adapts well to any soil or climate in Texas.

Pond Cypress.

Pond Cypress.

DOGWOOD
Cornus florida   Areas: 3, 4, 6

One of the most spectacular trees to use in Texas — especially in the sandy soil areas. Do not plant it in solid rock or alkaline clay. Dogwoods will do well if planted with azaleas in solid peat moss. Although they can adapt to a full-sun location, they are best when used as understory trees.

Dogwood.

Dogwood.

MEXICAN ELDER
Sambucus mexicana   Areas: 8

Mexican elder is a fast-growing tree that is seen only in the El Paso area. It has light, lime-green foliage and white flowers in the spring and summer. It is evergreen, but sometimes exhibits a slightly brownish cast in late summer.

Mexican Elder.

Mexican Elder.

Cedar Elm.

CEDAR ELM
Ulmus crassifolia   Areas: 1, 2, 3, 4, 5, 6, 7

Native to Texas, the cedar elm is an excellent shade tree choice. Drainage is not a big problem. The growth rate is fairly quick, and the transplant success rate is very high when the tree is moved in fall and winter months. It has fair yellow fall color. Cedar elm is also cost-effective since it grows wild in Texas. Typical elm problems don't affect this variety as much as other elms. So far, Dutch elm disease isn't a

54

problem and the elm leaf beetle will nibble on cedar elm only after the American, Siberian, and ascending elms have been gobbled up. (Ascending and Siberian elms are the worst choices for Dallas.) Cedar elm is relatively maintenance-free. Some pruning is required, but not every year; spraying for insects is rarely needed. The only problem with the cedar elm that I am somewhat concerned about is mildew, which has become worse in the past few years; spraying with benomyl in May will solve the problem, however.

CHINESE ELM (Lacebark Elm)
Ulmus parvifolia Areas: All

What many people mistakenly call the Chinese elm is actually the Siberian elm, a *terrible* variety that's dying out everywhere. The true Chinese, or Drake, elm is an excellent tree. It has small, shiny leaves and a mottled, light-colored bark. This tree has been used more in the Houston area than in any other part of Texas, but should be used more statewide.

GINKGO
Ginkgo biloba Areas: 2, 3, 4, 5, 6

The ginkgo is an excellent tree that grows almost anywhere. It has spectacular, yellow fall color, and very distinctive fan-shaped leaves. Best when planted in deep, rich soil. The ginkgo's only negative aspect is its extremely slow growth rate.

SAVANNAH HOLLY
Ilex opaca 'Savannah' Areas: 2, 3, 4, 5, 6

Savannah holly, East Palatka holly, and Foster holly are good alternatives to the standard yaupon holly that has been used so much in Texas.

Savannah has the most berries and larger multi-spined leaves. The East Palatka has slightly smaller leaves, one spine at the end of each leaf, and fewer berries. Foster holly has the smallest leaf of the three and dark green leaves.

DECIDUOUS YAUPON HOLLY
Ilex decidua Areas: 2, 3, 4, 5, 6

The deciduous yaupon or "possum haw" is native to Texas. It is widely available and often used as a

Cedar Elm.

Chinese Elm.

Chinese Elm.

Chinese Elm.

Ginkgo.

Ginkgo.

Savannah Holly.

Savannah Holly.

55

Deciduous Yaupon Holly.

Deciduous Yaupon Holly.

Deciduous Yaupon Holly.

Yaupon Holly.

Texas Mountain Laurel.

Honey Locust.

Magnolia.

Japanese Maple.

Bloodgood Japanese Maple.

decorative ornamental tree in sun or shade. Its foliage turns yellow and drops in fall, giving way to red berries that cover the branches for most of the winter. It is easy to transplant and very desirable.

YAUPON HOLLY
Ilex vomitoria   Areas: 2, 3, 4, 5, 6

This tree is a good choice if used properly. However, it is often used incorrectly in wide-open garden space. If used near a street or walkway, the yaupon holly should be placed in a raised planter, unless it is very large and high branching.

TEXAS MOUNTAIN LAUREL
Sophora secundiflora   Areas: 4, 5, 6

A small, dark green tree with fragrant violet flowers in the spring. It is slow-growing, but adapts nicely to dry soil conditions.

HONEY LOCUST
Gleditsia triacanthos   Areas: 1, 2, 6, 7

Its texture is quite light and graceful but, as a shade tree, it is a poor choice for most areas of Texas and is overrated. It has several insect problems.

MAGNOLIA
Magnolia grandiflora   Areas: 2, 3, 4, 5, 6

The magnolia is a very stately tree. It should be used as a focal point in the landscape. The magnolia is not a good shade tree. Nothing will grow under it, so it's best to let magnolia branches grow to the ground. This tree needs plenty of room.

JAPANESE MAPLE
Acer palmatum   Areas: All

Obviously high on my list of favorites, since I use it in almost every project, the Japanese maple has various forms and colors and provides interest year-round. Green varieties grow faster and larger but are less colorful than those like Bloodgood, which stays red during most of the growing season. The coral bark variety has bright red bark in the winter; the lacy leaf varieties are the smallest and are excellent used in pots. All have beautiful fall color. These maples are used mostly as understory trees but, when used in full sun, exhibit even better color.

MESQUITE

Prosopis glandulosa   Areas: All

Marked by a great branching structure, this native Texas tree has light, lacy foliage and can thrive in very dry parts of the state. To encourage the health of existing mesquite trees, avoid irrigating them.

BUR OAK

Quercus macrocarpa   Areas: All

A deciduous shade tree that grows very large and has a majestic branching characteristic, the bur oak should be used much more. The leaves are huge, sometimes a foot long, and the acorns are the size of a golf ball. Fall color is a so-so yellow. Many specimens live around the White Rock Creek area of Dallas. They grow very well in any soil as long as the drainage is positive.

CHINKAPIN OAK

Quercus muehlenbergi   Areas: 2, 3, 4, 6

The chinkapin oak grows native in Texas, but is seldom used as a landscape tree. That should change, because it's an excellent tree.

Huge specimens exist in various parts of the state. The chinkapin oak has light-colored bark, yellow fall color, and is fast-growing for an oak. The leaves are long ovals with serrated edges. It grows wild in some areas of Oklahoma. The chestnut oak is very similar, but doesn't grow as well in Texas. The serrated edge of the leaves has rounded points, contrasting with the chinkapin oak's sharp pointed edges.

LIVE OAK

Quercus virginiana   Areas: 3, 4, 5, 6

This is the slowest growing, most expensive, and most overused of the oaks. Native or field-collected live oaks are less expensive, but slower growing than nursery-grown live oaks. The '83-'84 freeze in Texas killed thousands of live oaks and severely damaged thousands more. (Some live oaks currently on the market may have latent freeze damage.) Live oaks require very high maintenance: pruning, cabling, and pampering. Live oaks are considered evergreens but they do drop their foliage in the spring when new growth appears.

Ribbonleaf Japanese Maple.

Coral Bark Japanese Maple.

Bur Oak.

Green Japanese Maple.

Bur Oak.

Mesquite.

Chinkapin Oak.

Chinkapin Oak.

Live Oak.

57

Red Oak.

Live Oak.

Red Oak.

Red Oak.

Pin oak leaf (top row); Shumard red oak leaf (bottom row)

Pin Oak — Avoid

Live oaks, until they are quite large, are stiff trees with little grace and no fall color. If you insist on planting live oaks, be sure to use underdrainage (a French-drain type system). When planted in consistently moist, poorly drained soil, live oaks will grow very little if at all. Live oaks should be used sparingly north of Waco.

RED OAK
Quercus shumardii Areas: 1, 2, 3, 4, 5, 6, 7

This is a great shade tree that grows naturally in Texas. A fast-growing oak, it requires little maintenance until it is very old. Fall color varies from brown to scarlet (so it is best to purchase red oak in the fall to see what color you are getting). Deciduous trees such as this not only have beautiful fall color, but they also let the sun shine through for warmth in winter.

There's one problem with the red oak: wet feet. Red oaks must have good positive drainage. Plant this tree on a slope or install drain lines at the depth of the bottom of the root ball. Most trees will live if they make it through the first year — not so with red oaks. If drainage is poor, they can die even in their second or third year; many older specimens have died when drainage problems have been created in their root zones. Red oaks will occasionally be plagued by borers, but they are usually a sign of stress brought on by another problem.

A very serious mix-up exists involving red oaks in Texas. A tree called the pin oak (Quercus palustris), shown at left, is being sold as the red oak all across the state. The specific red oak that the pin oak seems to be impersonating is Q. shumardii, which is an excellent tree for almost the entire state. In the past, this problem has been very difficult to detect since it was creeping into the marketplace so gently. It is my opinion that this mix-up is not intentional by any of the growers or contractors I've met. There seems to be a great amount of self-hybridization happening naturally, and the pin oak blood is accidentally turning up in the red oaks. I've seen the problem all over the country. The safest bet is to have the landscape contractor or nursery guarantee to replace the tree if the pin oak characteristics ever show up.

58

The pin oak is a rotten tree for Texas! If someone recommends it, don't even bother to discuss it with them. The pin oak is stiffer in character than the red oak, has a straight trunk, a pointed top, and a distinctive branching character. The top branches point up; the middle branches are horizontal; and all the low branches droop. Pin oak has smaller acorns than red oak, and the twigs are more flexible than red oak twigs.

The pin oak can be recognized easily in the summer in Texas by its yellow leaves with brown edges.

SAWTOOTH OAK
Quercus acutissima

Although unproven in Texas at this date, this tree shows early indications that it will be a winner. The few I know of that have been planted are alive and growing extremely fast for an oak. Sawtooth oak has a light-colored bark, long narrow leaves, and an open branching structure.

WATER OAK
Quercus nigra   Areas: 3, 4

The water oak is native to wet areas, but will adapt to well-drained soil if provided adequate moisture. This is probably the best shade tree to use in the Houston area. It does not do well in rock.

FAN PALM
Livistonia chinensis   Areas: 4, 5, 6

Slow-growing and wide-spreading, this is one of the best palms to grow in south Texas. It should be used to provide shade, particularly in very open areas of the landscape.

WASHINGTON PALM
Washingtonia robusta   Areas: 4, 5, 6

A taller-growing palm, the Washington variety is one of the best palms to use for landscape borders and near streets.

BRADFORD PEAR   Areas: 1, 2, 3, 4,
Pyrus calleryana 'Bradfordii'   5, 6, 7

This white-flowering ornamental tree has been used much more in Dallas during the last few years. Fast-growing and very healthy, this beautiful, small tree grows almost anywhere in the United States. Its fall color isn't consistent but, when good, is brilliant red.

Water Oak.

Sawtooth Oak

Water Oak.

Water Oak.

Fan Palm.

Washington Palm.

Bradford Pear.

Brad ford Pear.

59

Pecan.

Persimmon.

Persimmon.

Austrian Pine.

Eldarica Pine.

Japanese Black Pine.

Slash Pine.

PECAN
Carya illinoinensis Areas: All

I used to make the very foolish comment that pecans were too messy to use. Although they do get web-worms and have to be sprayed at times, pecans are low-maintenance, fast-growing shade trees that seem to live forever, becoming magnificent specimens. Sure, they drop some leaves and flowers on the ground, but so do all trees, to some extent. If you grow this tree for a pecan crop, your maintenance, naturally, will be higher.

PERSIMMON
Diospyros virginiana Areas: 2, 3, 4, 6

The persimmon is a graceful shade tree with attractive yellow fall color very early in the season. It should be used more in Texas. The fruit can be a little messy if branches grow over terraces. The bark is distinctively dark and deeply fissured.

AUSTRIAN PINE
Pinus nigra Areas: All

This is one of the best pines for clay soils. A wide-growing, dark green, healthy tree, the Austrian pine can be grown in most parts of Texas.

ELDARICA PINE
Pinus eldarica Areas: All

Frequently sold as the Mondell pine, this pine tree has gained greatly in popularity during the last few years due to its vigor and fast growth rate. The eldarica is upright in growth and retains its foliage to the ground, making it a good screen or property-line planting.

JAPANESE BLACK PINE
Pinus thunbergiana Areas: All

Another good pine for Texas, the Japanese black pine has a more irregular growth pattern and is usually more openly branched. Of the pines in this book, this one has the greatest tendency to develop chlorosis.

SLASH PINE
Pinus elliottii Areas: 2, 3, 4

The king of east Texas evergreen trees, this fast-growing pine is great in sandy soils, but worthless in most clay or alkaline soils. The slash pine always grows very straight. Other, similar varieties are loblolly and long-needle pines. Although the slash pine will grow in all the areas listed, it must be planted in sandy spots in those areas. Avoid alkaline clay soils at all costs.

CHINESE PISTACHIO
Pistacia chinensis   Areas: All

This is the best of the fast-growing trees. It will reach heights of 30 to 40 feet in less than 10 years. The delicate looking fall foliage ranges in color from yellow to deep red. I've seen absolutely no problems with the pistachio, and the availability is getting better each year. The largest specimens in Texas are about 60 feet tall with 36-inch calipers.

MEXICAN PLUM
Prunus mexicana   Areas: 2, 3, 4, 5, 6

The Mexican plum is a small, ornamental spring-flowering tree that is native to Texas. It should be used more as a landscape plant.

PURPLE PLUM
Prunus cerasifera   Areas: All

The purple plum is a lovely ornamental tree with pink blossoms in spring, and purple foliage all summer.

REDBUD
Cercis canadensis   Areas: 1, 2, 3, 4, 5, 6

The redbud is a good ornamental for spring color; it should be used as an understory tree.

Purple Plum.

Chinese Pistachio.

Chinese Pistachio.

Mexican Plum.

Chinese Pistachio.

Redbud.

Redbud.

Redbud.

61

Sweetgum

RUSSIANOLIVE
Elaeagnus angustifolia
Areas: All

A small to medium-sized, hardy tree that's excellent for dry areas. It is fast-growing and exhibits a distinctive gray green color.

SUMAC
Rhus typhina
Areas: 2, 3, 4, 5, 6

This bushy plant can be used as a shrub or small tree. It has beautiful, red, fall foliage and a very light branching structure; for maximum effect, it's best to use sumac with other plants. It can now be found in some nurseries or collected from the wild in Texas.

SWEETGUM
Liquidambar styraciflua
Areas: 2, 3, 4, 5, 6

Sweetgum trees are beginning to be used in great abundance in Texas. They are native to sandy soil areas of east Texas and Oklahoma. They do fine in most soils if a few rules are followed: do not plant in rock; do not plant on steep slopes; and give them plenty of water. They *can* be kept alive (and moderately healthy) in rock, but a regular application of sulphur and chelated iron is needed.

One of the self-pruning trees, with beautiful fall color and attractive branching structure in the winter, the sweetgum is a low-maintenance tree when planted in the right place. The fall color will sometimes be yellow, salmon, scarlet, and maroon — all on the same tree at the same time. Some just turn yellow; I'm still trying to find out why. Some people think the spiny fruit balls are a problem, but I don't.

DESERT WILLOW
Chilopsis linearis
Areas: 4, 5, 6, 7, 8

With its lacy foliage, interesting branching structure, and lavender-to-pink flowers in the summer, the desert willow is an excellent small tree for dry areas.

Sweetgum.

Russianolive.

Sumac.

Desert Willow.

Easy Reference Tree Chart

Growth rates and mature sizes are given to compare relative statistics among types; these statistics are not absolutes and may vary from city to city within one area.

	ASH	CRAB APPLE	CRAPE MYRTLE	BALD CYPRESS	POND CYPRESS	DOGWOOD	MEXICAN ELDER	CEDAR ELM
Areas	All	All	2-3-4-5-6	2-3-4-5-6	2-3-4-5-6	3-4-6	8	1-2-3-4-5-6-7
Use	Shade, Fall Color	Orn.	Orn., Color	Shade	Shade	Orn. Understory	Shade, Orn.	Shade
Type	D	D	D	D	D	D	E	D
Fall Color	Yellow to Red	Yellow to Red	Yellow and Red	Reddish Brown	Reddish Brown	Red	Green	Yellow
Summer Color	Medium Green	Medium Green	Medium Green	Light Green	Light Green	Dark Green	Lime Green	Medium Green
Flowers	—	Pink, Red, White	White, Pink, Red, Lav.	—	—	Pink, White	White	—
Mature Height	60'	15'	15'	70'	80'	20'	20'	50'
Maximum Height	80'	25'	25'	120'	120'	35'	30'	80'
Annual Growth Rate	12-18"	6-8"	4-6"	10-12"	2-3'	6-8"	12-15"	6-9"
Mature Spread	40'	20'	15'	30'	25'	20'	25'	40'
Exposure	Sun	Sun	Sun	Sun	Sun	Shade/ Pt. Shade	Sun	Sun
Soil	All	All	All	All	All	Sandy, Acid	All	All
Availability	Excellent	Good	Good	Very Good	Poor	Good	Good	Excellent
Possible Problems	Insects	Short Lived, Diseases	Insects, Mildew, Freeze	None	None	Soil Problems in Clay	None	Mildew

LEGEND:
D = Deciduous   Orn. = Ornamental   Pt. = Partial
E = Evergreen   Prep. = Prepared

	CHINESE ELM	GINKGO	SAVANNAH HOLLY	DECIDUOUS YAUPON HOLLY	YAUPON HOLLY	TEXAS MOUNTAIN LAUREL	HONEY LOCUST	MAGNOLIA
Areas	All	2-3-4-5-6	2-3-4-5-6	2-3-4-5-6	2-3-4-5-6	4-5-6	1-2-6-7	2-3-4-5-6
Design Use	Shade	Shade, Fall Color	Orn. (Winter Berries)	Orn. (Winter Berries)	Orn. (Winter Berries)	Orn.	Shade	Specimen
Type	D	D	E	D	E	E	D	E
Fall Color	Yellow	Yellow	Green	Yellow	Green	Green	Yellow	Green
Summer Color	Medium-Dark Green	Medium Green	Medium Green	Medium Green	Medium Green	Dark Green	Dark Green	Dark Green
Flowers	—	—	Small White, Pink	Small White	Small White	Violet	—	White
Mature Height	50'	50'	15'	15'	15'	20'	50'	50'
Maximum Height	60'	70'	40'	20'	25'	30'	80'	75'
Annual Growth Rate	8-12"	4-6"	4-6"	4-6"	4-6"	4-6"	6-12"	6-8"
Mature Spread	40'	30'	20'	15'	15'	15'	50'	30'
Exposure	Sun	Sun	Sun/Pt. Shade	Sun/Pt. Shade	Sun/Pt. Shade	Shade/Pt. Shade	Sun	Sun
Soil	All	All	All but Rock	All	All	All	All	All but Solid Rock
Availability	Good	Good	Fair	Fair	Excellent	Fair	Good	Excellent
Possible Problems	None	Slow Growth, Heat	None	None	None	Hard to Transplant	Insects	Messy, Needs Space

	JAPANESE MAPLE	MESQUITE	BUR OAK	CHINKAPIN OAK	LIVE OAK	RED OAK	WATER OAK	FAN PALM
Areas	All	All	All	2-3-4-6	3-4-5-6	1-2-3-4-6-7	3-4	4-5-6
Design Use	Specimen, Understory	Shade	Shade	Shade	Shade	Shade	Shade	Orn., Specimen
Type	D	D	D	D	E	D	D	E
Fall Color	Orange to Red	Yellow	Dark Yellow	Dark Yellow	Green	Yellow, Orange, Red, Brown	Pale Yellow	Green
Summer Color	Dark Green to Red	Medium Green	Dark Green	Medium Green	Dark Green	Dark Green	Dark Green	Medium Green
Flowers	—	—	—	—	—	—	—	—
Mature Height	12'	20'	50'	50'	50'	60'	60'	30'
Maximum Height	20'	30'	80'	80'	80'	90'	100'	40'
Annual Growth	4-6"	6-8"	9-12"	9-12"	4-6"	12-18"	9-12"	6-8"
Mature Spread	20'	40'	50'	60'	70'	80'	50'	15'
Exposure	Shade/ Pt. Shade	Sun	Sun	Sun	Sun	Sun	Sun	Sun
Soil	All	All but Wet	All	All	All	All	Deep, Neutral to Acid	All
Availability	Very Good	Fair	Fair	Poor	Very Good	Very Good	Very Good	Good
Possible Problems	None	Wet Soil	Wet Feet	None	Freeze, Pruning	Wet Feet	Alkalinity	Wet Soil

	WASHINGTON PALM	BRADFORD PEAR	PECAN	PERSIMMON	AUSTRIAN PINE	ELDARICA PINE	JAPANESE BLACK PINE	SLASH PINE
Areas	4-5-6	1-2-3-4-5-6-7	All	2-3-4-6	All	All	All	2-3-4
Design Use	Orn., Specimen	Orn.	Shade, Crop	Shade	Orn.	Screening, Specimen	Orn.	Shade
Type	E	D	D	D	E	E	E	E
Fall Color	Green	Red	Yellow	Yellow	Green	Green	Green	Green
Summer Color	Medium Green	Dark Green	Dark Green	Medium Green	Dark Green	Dark Green	Dark Green	Medium Green
Flowers	—	White	—	—	—	—	—	—
Mature Height	50'	25'	60'	30'	30'	30'	20'	60'
Maximum Height	80'	30'	100'	60'	50'	40'	40'	90'
Annual Growth Rate	12"	9-10"	12"	9-12"	6"	2-3"	6"	2-3'
Mature Spread	12'	20'	70'	35'	15'	20'	10'	25'
Exposure	Sun	Sun	Sun	Sun	Sun		Sun	Sun
Soil	All	All	All	All	All	All	All	Sandy, Acid
Availability	Good	Excellent	Good	Poor	Good	Good	Very Good	Excellent
Possible Problems	Wet Soil	Cotton Root Rot	Webworms	Webworms	Chlorosis, Insects	Insects	Chlorosis, Insects	Alkaline Soil, Insects

	CHINESE PISTACHIO	MEXICAN PLUM	PURPLE PLUM	REDBUD	RUSSIAN-OLIVE	SUMAC	SWEETGUM	DESERT WILLOW
Areas	All	2-3-4-5-6	All	1-2-3-4-5-6	All	2-3-4-5-6	2-3-4-5-6	4-5-6-7-8
Design Use	Shade	Orn.	Orn.	Orn. Understory	Orn., Shade	Orn.	Shade, Fall Color	Orn. Shade
Type	D	D	D	D	D	D	D	D
Fall Color	Yellow to Salmon	Yellow	Purple	Yellow	Yellow	Red	Maroon to Yellow	Yellow
Summer Color	Medium Green	Medium Green	Purple to Green	Dark Green	Gray Green	Dark Green	Dark Green	Medium Green
Flowers	—	White in Spring	Pink	White, Purple	—	White	—	Pink to Lavender
Mature Height	40'	20'	15'	20'	20'	10'	60'	25'
Maximum Height	70'	30'	20'	35'	30'	15'	90'	30'
Annual Growth Rate	18-24"	6-8"	4-6"	6-8"	6-8"	4"	6-9"	6-8"
Mature Spread	25'	20'	10'	25'	20'	15'	30'	25'
Exposure	Sun	Sun	Sun or Shade	Sun/Pt. Shade	Sun	Sun	Sun	Sun
Soil	All	All	All	All	All	All	All	All
Availability	Fair	Poor	Very Good	Red-Excel. White-Fair	Good	Fair	Excellent	Fair
Possible Problems	None	None	None	Insects	Wet Soil	None	Chlorosis	Wet Soil

TREES TO AVOID

I recommend that you do *not* plant these trees:

1. **Mulberry** — has bad roots and ugly foliage.

2. **Mimosa** — has bad roots and is plagued by diseases.

3. **Sycamore** — has diseases, messy foliage, and damaging roots (although I love the white trunks of the natives).

4. **Hackberry** — is short-lived; has ugly foliage and brittle wood.

5. **Poplar** — is plagued by insects and diseases; is short-lived (though silver poplar is pretty good).

6. **American Elm** — is grand when healthy, but is susceptible to the usual elm problems.

7. **Siberian Elm** — mistakenly called Chinese Elm; the Siberian is just awful.

8. **Cottonwood** — is brittle, messy, and has damaging roots.

9. **Chinese Tallow** — is susceptible to freeze damage; has brittle wood; is plagued by cotton root rot.

10. **Pin Oak** — chlorosis in alkaline soils and cross pollination with red oaks.

SOME GENERAL TREE TIPS:

1. **Do not flush-cut when pruning.** Leave a slight stub so the collar can begin its natural healing process.

2. **Do not paint cuts.** It's a waste of money and slows the healing process just like a bandage acts on a cut finger.

3. **Do not prune off lower limbs.** "Raising" the branching structure to exaggerated heights looks bad and puts serious stress on trees.

4. **Do not top, dehorn or bob-back trees.** Never inflict these procedures on any trees, especially crape myrtles.

5. **Fence off the root zone.** During hard construction, do this to protect trees from traffic, stored materials, etc.

6. **Avoid cutting or filling a tree's root zone.** It will smother the tree.

7. **Dig root balls** to a width of at least 9 inches per 1 inch of trunk caliper. In other words, a 4-inch caliper tree should have a ball that's at least 36 inches in diameter.

8. **Do not stake trees.** If the ball size is large enough and has the proper amount of soil, tree staking is not necessary. In addition, staking weakens and girdles trees.

9. **Backfill with existing soil.** Do not add soil amendments.

Shrubs

In many cases, shrubs help to fill out and finish a good landscape plan, but I would warn you not to use more than is necessary. They are very expensive per square foot of landscaped area and are susceptible to insect and disease damage and freezing temperatures.

Recommended planting areas are noted below each of the following photographs of shrubs.

Aralia.
Areas: 4, 5, 6

Azaleas.
Areas: 2, 3, 4, 5, 6

Dwarf Bamboo.
Areas: 3, 4, 5, 6

Barberry.
Areas: All

Cyperus.
Areas: 3, 4, 5, 6

Elaeagnus.
Areas: All

Bamboo.
Areas: 3, 4, 5, 6

Bottlebrush.
Areas: 4, 5, 6

Wood Fern.
Areas: 2, 3, 4, 5, 6

Fountain Grass.
Areas: All

Pampas Grass.
Areas: All

Indian Hawthorn.
Areas: All

Dwarf Burford Holly.
Areas: 2, 3, 4, 5, 6

Dwarf Chinese Holly.
Areas: 2, 3, 4, 5, 6

Nellie R. Stevens Holly.
Areas: 2, 3, 4, 5, 6

Dwarf Yaupon Holly.
Areas: 2, 3, 4, 5, 6

Junipers.
Areas: All

Horsetail.
Areas: All

Italian Jasmine.
Areas: All

Lotus.
Areas: All

Dwarf Crape Myrtle.
Areas: 3, 4, 5, 6

Spirea.
Areas: All

Compact Nandina.
Areas: All

Oleander.
Areas: 4, 5, 6

Photinia Fraseri.
Areas: All

Sago Palm.
Areas: 4, 5, 6

Pittosporum.
Areas: 4, 5, 6

Senecia.
Areas: All

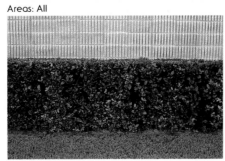

Sumac:
Areas: All

Yucca.
Areas: All

Viburnum.
Areas: 3, 4, 5, 6

Natal Plum.
Areas: 4, 5, 6

Easy Reference Shrub Chart

Growth rates and mature sizes are given to compare relative statistics among types; these statistics are not absolutes, and may vary from city to city within one area.

	ARALIA	AZALEA	BAMBOO	DWARF BAMBOO	BARBERRY	BOTTLE-BRUSH	CYPERUS	ELAEAGNUS
Areas	4-5-6	2-3-4-5-6	3-4-5-6	3-4-5-6	All	4-5-6	3-4-5-6	All
Design Use	Specimen, Mass	Mass	Barrier, Screen	Mass, Ground Cover	Mass	Specimen, Screen	Specimen, Aquatic	Hedge, Mass
Type	E	E	E	E	Semi-E	E	D	E
Flowers	—	All colors	—	—	Yellow	White, Red	—	White
Spacing	36-42"	3-5'	3-6'	12-24"	24-40"	3-6'	24-36"	3-5'
Exposure	Shade	Shade/Pt. Shade	Sun/Pt. Shade	Sun/Pt. Shade	Sun/Pt. Shade	Sun	Sun/Pt. Shade	Sun or Shade
Soil	Prep.	Solid Peat Moss	All	All	Prep.	All	All	All
Possible Problems	Freeze, Insects	Alkalinity, Dry Climate	Spreading	Spreading	Thorns	None	None	Fast Growth

	WOOD FERN	FOUNTAIN GRASS	PAMPAS GRASS	INDIAN HAWTHORN	DWARF BURFORD HOLLY	DWARF CHINESE HOLLY	NELLIE R. STEVENS HOLLY	DWARF YAUPON HOLLY
Areas	2-3-4-5-6	All	All	All	2-3-4-5-6	2-3-4-5-6	2-3-4-5-6	2-3-4-5-6
Design Use	Mass	Mass, Color	Mass, Color	Hedge, Mass	Hedge, Mass	Hedge, Mass	Hedge, Screen, Specimen	Hedge, Mass
Type	D	D	D	E	E	E	E	E
Flowers	—	White, Purple	White	White, Pink	—	—	—	—
Spacing	18-24"	36-48"	8-10'	24-36"	24-36"	18-30"	36-54"	24-36"
Exposure	Shade to Pt. Shade	Sun	Sun	Sun/Pt. Shade	Sun, Shade	Sun, Shade	Sun, Shade	Sun, Shade
Soil	All	All	All	Prep.	Prep.	Prep.	All	Prep.
Possible Problems	None	None	None	Disease	Insects	Insects	None	Insects

	HORSETAIL	ITALIAN JASMINE	JUNIPER	LOTUS	DWARF CRAPE MYRTLE	COMPACT NANDINA	OLEANDER	SAGO PALM
Areas	All	3-4-5-6	All	All	3-4-5-6	3-4-5-6	4-5-6	4-5-6
Design Use	Aquatic	Hedge, Mass	Hedge, Mass	Aquatic	Hedge, Color	Hedge, Mass	Specimen, Hedge, Screen	Specimen
Type	D	Semi-E	E	D	D	E	E	E
Flowers	—	Yellow	—	All Colors	White, Red, Pink, Purple	—	Red, White, Pink	—
Spacing	24-36"	36-42"	36-42"	24"-8'	3-6'	24-36"	5-6'	6-8'
Exposure	Sun, Pt. Sun	Sun	Sun	Sun	Sun	Sun, Shade	Sun	Sun
Soil	Water	Prep.	All	Water	All	All	All	Acid
Possible Problems	None	Freeze	Insects	None	None	None	Freeze	Freeze

	PHOTINIA	PITTO-SPORUM	NATAL PLUM	SENECIA	SPIREA	SUMAC	VIBURNUM	YUCCA
Areas	All	4-5-6	4-5-6	All	All	All	3-4-5-6	All
Design Use	Hedge, Screen	Hedge, Mass	Hedge, Mass	Hedge, Mass, Color	Hedge, Color	Color, Specimen	Hedge, Screen	Mass, Specimen
Type	E	E	E	E	D	D	E	E
Flowers	White	—	White	Violet	White	—	White	Red, White
Spacing	5-6'	24-42"	24-36"	24-42"	36-48"	8-10'	42-54"	3-5'
Exposure	Sun/ Pt. Shade	Sun/ Pt. Shade	Sun	Sun	Sun	Sun	Sun/ Pt. Shade	Sun
Soil	All	Prep.	Prep.	All	All	All	Prep.	All
Possible Problems	None	Freeze	Freeze	None	None	None	Freeze	None

Ground Covers and Vines

These are spoken of together because many of the plants will both climb and serve as a low ground cover.

Ground covers such as English ivy and Asian jasmine are lower maintenance in some areas (especially in shade) than grass. Offsetting that advantage is the fact that the initial expense for these ground covers is much greater than grass. Not only do the plants cost more, but also the bed preparation for ground covers is more involved and more costly than for grass.

Vining plants give a fast, inexpensive, fun effect. Some climb by clinging to any surface (English ivy, Boston ivy, fig ivy, etc.); others must be supported by wire or a trellis (Carolina jessamine, clematis, grapes, etc.).

Recommended planting areas are noted beneath each of the following photographs of ground covers and vines.

Bougainvillea.
Areas: 5

Coyote Bush.
Areas: 8

Clematis.
Areas: 3, 4, 5

Euonymus coloratus.
Areas: 2, 3, 4

Honeysuckle.
Areas: All

Algerian Ivy.
Areas: 2, 3, 4, 5

Boston Ivy.
Areas: All

Fig Ivy.
Areas: 3, 4, 5

Boston Ivy.
Areas: All

74

English Ivy.
Areas: All

Lady Banksia Rose.
Areas: All

Gill Ivy.
Areas: 2, 3, 4, 5

Asian Jasmine.
Areas.: 3, 4, 5

Confederate Jasmine.
Areas: 3, 4, 5

Carolina Jessamine.
Areas: 1, 2, 3, 4, 5, 6

Wilton Juniper.
Areas: All

Liriope.
Areas: 1, 2, 3, 4, 5, 6

Ophiopogon.
Areas: 2, 3, 4, 5, 6

Rosemary.
Areas: 1, 2, 3, 6, 7, 8

Sedum.
Areas: 2, 3, 4, 5, 6

Mock Strawberries.
Areas: 2, 3, 4, 5, 6

Trumpet Vine.
Areas: All

Silver-Lace Vine.
Areas: 1, 2, 6, 7, 8

Wisteria.
Areas: 1, 2, 3, 4, 5, 6, 7

Virginia Creeper.
Areas: All

Easy Reference Ground Cover and Vine Chart

Growth rates and mature sizes are given to compare relative statistics among types; these statistics are not absolutes, and may vary from city to city within one area.

	BOUGAIN-VILLEA	CLEMATIS	COYOTE BRUSH	EUONYMUS COLORATUS	HONEY-SUCKLE	ALGERIAN IVY	BOSTON IVY	ENGLISH IVY
Areas	5	3-4-5	8	2-3-4	All	2-3-4-5	All	All
Design Use	Vine	Vine	Ground Cover	Ground Cover	Ground Cover/ Vine	Vine	Vine	Cover/ Vine
Type	E	D	E	E	E	E	D	E
Flowers	All Colors	All colors	White, Yellow	—	White/ Purple	—	—	—
Spacing	3-15'	3-6'	12-30"	12-18"	18-24" GC 5-7' Vine	24"-5'	3-15' Vine	3-5' Vine
Exposure	Sun	Sun	Sun	Sun/ Pt. Shade	Sun/ Shade	Shade	Sun/ Shade	Shade/ Pt. Shade
Soil	Prep.	Prep.	Prep.	Prep.	All	Prep.	All	Prep.
Possible Problems	Freeze	Heat	None	Insects	None	Insects	Heat	Heat

	FIG IVY	GILL IVY	ASIAN JASMINE	CONF. JASMINE	CAROLINA JESSAMINE	WILTON JUNIPER	LIRIOPE	OPHIOPOGON
Areas	3-4-5	2-3-4-5	3-4-5	3-4-5	1-2-3-4-5-6	All	2-3-4-5-6	2-3-4-5-6
Design Use	Vine	Ground Cover	Ground Cover	Vine	Vine	Ground Cover	Ground Cover	Ground Cover
Type	E	E	E	E	E	E	E	E
Flowers	—	—	—	Yellow	Yellow	—	Purple	E
Spacing	3-5'	12-24"	9-18"	3-5'	4-10'	18-36"	9-18"	9-12"
Exposure	Sun/Pt. Shade	Shade	Sun/Shade	Sun/Shade	Sun/Shade	Sun	Sun/Shade	Sun/Shade
Soil	All	All	Prep.	Prep.	Prep.	All	All	Prep.
Possible Problems	Freeze	Heat	Freeze	Freeze	Freeze	Insects	None	Insects

	LADY BANKSIA ROSE	ROSEMARY	SEDUM	MOCK STRAW-BERRY	SILVER-LACE VINE	TRUMPET VINE	VIRGINIA CREEPER	WISTERIA
Areas	All	1-2-3-6-7-8	2-3-4-5-6	2-3-4-5-6	1-2-6-7-8	All	All	1-2-3-4-5-6-7
Design Use	Vine	Ground Cover	Ground Cover	Ground Cover	Vine	Vine	Vine	Vine
Type	Semi-E	E	E	E	D	D	D	D
Flowers	White/Yellow	Purple	Yellow/Red	White	White	Yellow/Red	—	Purple/White
Spacing	4-8'	12-24"	6-12"	9-12"	5-8'	6-12'	5-8'	8-10'
Exposure	Sun	Sun	Sun/Pt. Shade	Sun	Sun	Sun/Shade	Sun	Sun
Soil	All	All	Prep.	Prep.	All	Prep.	All	All
Possible Problems	None	None	None	Insects	Heat	Fast Growth	Fast Growth	Fast Growth

UNDERGROUND DRAINAGE
Advantage: Reasonable cost.
Disadvantage: Must have adequate grade change to allow water to drain away from site.

MOUNDED BED
Advantage: Minimal cost.
Disadvantage: Highest maintenance.

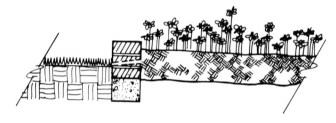

RETAINED BED
Advantages: Reduced maintenance; most permanent.
Disadvantage: Most expensive.

Flowers

Flowers are the finishing touches in the garden. Since most varieties are temporary, they are the most flexible landscape elements.

Most flowers will grow in Texas at some time of the year; the following are particularly good for our state:

Ageratum	Iris
Alyssum	Lantana
Aster	Marigold
Begonia	Pansy
Caladium	Periwinkle
Candytuft	Petunia
Chrysanthemum	Plumbago
Copperleaf	Portulaca
Daffodil	Purslane
Daisy	Rose
Daylily	Snapdragon
Geranium	Thrift
Hibiscus	Tulip
Hypericum	Verbena
Impatiens	Zinnia

THE RAISED FLOWER BED

Flowers, annuals, and perennials require better soil than other plant materials. A very loose, sandy soil with lots of organic material (peat moss or compost) is best.

Flowers also need excellent drainage, which can be provided in three ways: underground drainage (PVC pipe in gravel), mounded beds, or raised beds that use some kind of retaining wall. Each type has its advantages and disadvantages, which are noted below. The depth of the prepared soil should be at least 12 inches.

Above: Ageratum, Begonia, Periwinkle.

Left: Spoon-petaled Mums.

78

Alyssum.

Asters.

Candytuft.

Caladiums.

Copperleaf and Periwinkle.

Daisy.

Daffodil and Pansy.

Daylily.

Geranium.

Hibiscus with Cactus.

Hypericum.

Impatiens.

Iris.

Mum.

Purslane.

Thrift.

Petunia.

Lantana.

Marigold.

Tulip.

Plumbago.

Portulaca.

Rose.

Snapdragon.

Verbena.

Zinnia.

Lawn Grasses

The two most commonly used grasses in Texas are St. Augustine and common Bermuda grass. The Bermuda grass does best in full sun; St. Augustine is the best grass for shady areas.

Bermuda grass should be seeded, hydromulched, or put in solid sod. Seeding is cheapest; hydromulching is the most efficient method; solid sod is most expensive, but gives you an instant lawn.

St. Augustine can be plugged or sprigged, but these are very unsatisfactory methods and should be avoided. Research is still being done on producing seed from this grass, but it isn't on the market yet. Planting solid sod is the best method. Usually you'll find some Bermuda grass in the St. Augustine sod. What happens is that the Bermuda takes over in sunny spots, and the St. Augustine takes over in the shady spots.

The cold winters of the early 1980's killed a large amount of St. Augustine, so be careful when using it in the northern parts of the state.

Zoysia grasses are gaining in popularity in Texas and are especially good for use on slopes and in small or narrow places. Since the grass spreads so slowly, it must be planted in a solid mass. The advantage of this grass is that you'll have fewer mowing and weeding chores, and lower edging costs. Meyer, which is the larger-leafed variety, is my favorite. Emerald and Tenefolia are smaller-leafed varieties. Tenefolia may freeze in the northern parts of the state.

Tif grasses, which are hybrids of common Bermuda grass, are beautiful, but high maintenance. Tifs are classified by the size of the leaf blade. Tif 419 is the largest and is often used on golf-course tees and fairways. Tif 328 is the variety used for Bermuda putting greens. The smallest is dwarf tif, which is still sometimes used for putting green surfaces, although not as often as 328.

Cool-season grasses include rye, fescue, bent, and blue. Bent grass is the premier putting-green grass; perennial rye is a favorite grass for overseeding Bermuda in the fall for winter color. Perennial rye seems to have a less toxic effect on the Bermuda when it returns the following spring. Having a mix of grasses has never bothered me; my lawn is a mix of about 15 different grasses.

Finishing Touches

Furniture and Accessories

Furniture and accessories — pots, statuary, wind chimes, etc. — are important finishing touches to the garden design. Furnishings, especially, should be kept simple and be comfortable, since these elements are to be used first, seen second.

Walter Lamb Furniture, terra-cotta pots with mums, and a ceramic ashtray.

Mailboxes should be subtle and, of course, functional.

Wood benches can be functional and serve as a sculptural focal point.

(Below) Garden room created by removing walls of maid's quarters. Accessories include potted plants, antique furniture, and glass and wicker coffee table. Dog run outside window.

Tree grates can increase the usable area of a terrace or walk.

Small trees (such as this Japanese maple) can also be used in pots.

Potted annual color can be effective if not overdone. Don't mix and match plants or pots.

Wind chimes are a visual and audible experience.

Garden sculpture can be elaborate and expensive or whimsical and inexpensive.

White swan and ducks. Animation from wildlife is a pleasant garden addition.

Turtle and Japanese koi.

Comfortable wrought-iron furniture, iron-duck shoe scraper, and potted jasmine.

Painted aluminum furniture is attractive, but can be uncomfortable.

Lighting

Landscape lighting stretches the enjoyment of gardens into the nighttime hours and also provides an effective level of security. Lighting should be designed so that light and dark spaces work in contrast to create interest and show off the depth of the garden. Lighting the entire garden area evenly is boring and a waste of money.

Lighting designed sensitively with the overall landscape plan can help to create one of the most relaxing and enjoyable aspects of the garden design.

Uplights are primarily for illuminating trees and vertical surfaces. Downlights illuminate the ground plane and cast interesting shadows on the ground. Twinkle lights and flood lights are used primarily for decorative purposes.

Mercury vapor lights are most commonly used for landscape lighting. They produce a pleasantly spreading moonlight effect and are economical to burn. These lights are usually 100 watt or 175 watt, depending on the size of the area to be lighted. A less powerful light is the small 504 bullet with a blue-white incandescent lamp.

The most important thing to remember about landscape lighting is that the lighting itself is not the product: the product is the illuminated garden. Lighting that doesn't blend into the overall garden design and become part of the total composition is a failure.

I would recommend avoiding the small, multi-colored, low-voltage lights. They are cheap looking and do nothing to enhance the garden design.

Pole lights are used for large areas.

Tree-mounted uplight.

504 mini-incandescent tree downlights.

(Top) Illuminated garden.

(Left) Recessed uplight.

(Right, center) Tree downlight.

(Right, bottom) Tree-mounted floodlight.

Illuminated garden.

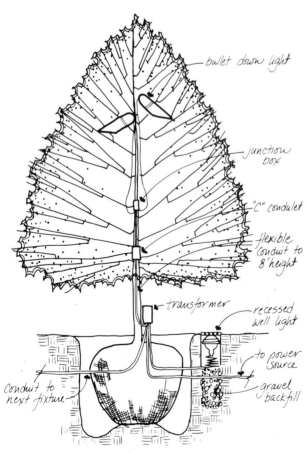

bullet down light

junction box

"C" condulet

flexible conduit to 8' height

transformer

recessed well light

to power source

conduit to next fixture

gravel backfill

TREE LIGHTING DETAIL

IV. *Maintaining Your Landscape*

Maintenance as a Design Tool

$\mathcal{P}$oor maintenance can ruin a well-designed garden. Good maintenance can make even a poorly designed garden attractive. Good design, together with proper maintenance, is, of course, the most successful combination.

Maintenance is not just a functional requirement that keeps a garden from growing out of control. It is another important design tool that is used to preserve and enhance garden spaces.

Pruning

The pruning of plants is one part of maintenance that is very much a design function. Limbs of trees can be lifted and trimmed symmetrically to create a formal effect, or they can be left low, sweeping, and asymmetrical to maintain a soft, more natural look.

So many beautiful shrubs and trees have been butchered around Texas that it is a shame. There exists a strong desire in many people (usually husbands home on the weekends) to hack shrubs and small trees into straight lines, blobs, and rectangular disasters. When asked why they are performing this ritual, these

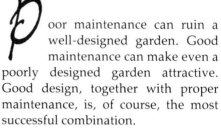
Improper flush cut leaving no collar.

Proper cut showing collar preserved.

Improper cut leaving too much stub.

A properly pruned shade tree.

An uplifted tree, a bad pruning technique.

88

"hackers" respond the same way they do when asked why they spread sandy loam on their lawns: "Well, I saw other people doing it." Brilliant! Does that mean that if a hacker saw someone jump off a cliff, he would take the plunge too?

Although good pruning practices have increased, very little proper pruning is being done with attention to aesthetics and plant health.

An excellent time to prune is fall, because problems can be more easily seen while the leaves are still on the trees. Pruning can be done at anytime during the year, however, summer pruning is dangerous since diseases may spread.

When you do prune, use clean, sharp tools to remove dead wood, suckers, and broken or badly bruised branches. And, to promote the tree's healing process, make no flush cuts, and do not use tree paint.

There are three basic steps in the pruning procedure:
1. Remove dead wood and mistletoe.
2. Remove damaged and weak wood, such as suckers and limbs that rub.
3. Selectively remove a portion of limbs and foliage throughout the tree to allow light shafts to enter. This is necessary only on trees that develop very dense canopies.

Cabling (wire supports on tree limbs) should be avoided in most cases. The only time I use cabling is when damage has occurred and repair is necessary. Cabling simply moves the weak spot from point A to point B, robs the tree of its natural tensile strength, and opens wounds where the bolts are inserted.

Cultivating

To greatly increase the establishment of new plant material, rough lightly the surface of bare spots in planting beds on a regular basis, at least once every two weeks. This procedure allows more oxygen to reach the root system, allows water to penetrate better, and keeps weeds to a minimum.

Mulching

Mulching is the placement of material on the bare spots in new planting sites. This process is perfect for the somewhat lazy gardener, since it eliminates the need for regular cultivation during establishment. Mulching also controls weeds, holds the moisture in the ground, and keeps the soil surface cooler.

Mulches include peat moss, compost, pine needles, and bark. Large size (3 to 5 inch) deco bark is my favorite, since it locks into place better than the other materials.

Pine needles make a good mulch, but should be used only in parts of the state where pine trees grow, or else the needles look out of place. Sometimes, gravel can be used as mulch. *Never* use plastic sheets as mulch, or for anything else in the garden. The worst of its many bad points is that it smothers the roots and will kill the plant.

Fertilizing

Trees can usually be fertilized by simply fertilizing the surrounding

Cultivation tool and turning fork.

Overpruned, deformed trees.

Dehorned crape myrtles.

grass or planting areas at the rate of 20 pounds per 1,000 square feet, using a solution with a 3-1-2 ratio. Putting the fertilizer into holes around the trees is necessary only in areas where the fertilizer may wash away. Newly planted trees should not be fertilized the first year. Always base the rate of application on the square footage of area to be covered rather than on the caliper inches of each tree trunk. Too, be sure to water thoroughly after any fertilizer application.

Trees, shrubs and ground covers should be fertilized four times per year (in March, June, October, and December) at 20 pounds per 1,000 square feet. Use a solution with a 3-1-2 ratio; apply and lightly cultivate into the soil. Water thoroughly after fertilizing.

Azaleas and camellias should be fertilized after the blooms have fallen from the plants and again in late summer. Following package directions, use any standard brand of special acidifying azalea-and-camellia fertilizer. Water thoroughly after application.

Watering

Gardens should be watered enough to keep the soil slightly moist, never constantly wet or boggy.

In very general terms, the following schedule applies:

Winter Months: 1 watering per week (including grass areas)

Spring and Fall: 2 waterings per week

Summer Months: 1 watering every other day

Newly Planted Material: 1 watering per day in summer, 1 watering per week in winter months.

Obviously, clouds, rain, snow, drainage, water bills, type of watering (automatic or by hand), and length of watering time all affect this schedule. I suggest, initially, that you follow this watering schedule, and then adjust it to reach the moisture level desired in the various areas of your gardens.

Newly planted trees should be thoroughly soaked once per week in the hot growing season, and twice per month in the cooler seasons. This should be done in addition to regular watering of the grass areas or planting areas surrounding the trees. Once trees are established, a regular watering of the surrounding planting areas should suffice. During periods of extreme drought, however, the soaking procedure may need to be repeated.

Shrubs should be watered according to the tree-watering instructions above. However, newly planted shrubs can dry out very quickly during the hot summer months, and should be checked daily. The amount of full sun, drainage, and type of soil may necessitate daily watering.

Ground covers should be watered every day during the first growing season. This is extremely important due to the small root systems of these plants. Once established, ground covers require about the same amount of water as grass. A warning: If the sprinkler system is used often enough to quench the thirst of newly planted ground cover, shrubs and trees in the area may drown; therefore, a light hand-watering of ground covers is usually necessary during the first season to supplement the sprinkler system.

Annuals and potted plants should be watered daily through the hot months and as needed during the cooler months. Once the plants have filled in solidly, use the same watering schedule as the rest of the garden.

Grass watering in the winter months is very important to prevent dieback from desiccation. During dry windy periods, water once per week. In the summer, water lawn areas at least three times per week.

Root systems of almost all plants need slow, deep watering, and the foliage needs the humidity and the cleaning action of sprinkling . . . so use both!

GENERAL MAINTENANCE RULES:
1. Water carefully and consistently (especially during the first year).
2. Mow and edge regularly, and catch and remove the clippings.
3. Keep bare areas of planting sites lightly cultivated until plants fill out.
4. Keep your garden clean at all times.

V. *Case Studies*

Residential Projects

Residential gardens should be fun, beautiful, maintainable, and flexible; other than that, your choices are wide open. The palette of plants, art, and hard-construction elements is plentiful, and should be used liberally but wisely.

If you are working with a landscape expert who suggests that he or she knows everything, it's time to change to someone else or do the work yourself, because no one knows everything about landscape design; nature is simply too huge and varied.

Residential landscape design is the most personal form of this art. Personal involvement with the client and the attention to detail is extensive, since the owner tends to offer the designer free, round-the-clock site inspection.

This section of the book shows completed gardens that range widely in style, scope, and cost. Hopefully, you will be able to use some of the solutions in your garden — or better yet, be inspired to come up with even better ideas of your own.

(Above) Back garden area.

(Right) View of front yard plantings.

An English Garden in Texas

This project was a redo of an existing property. Although it was an older, established landscape, it had few existing trees. That made the introduction of trees a high priority. New planting beds were added to blend with the quaint architecture.

The front garden uses large trees on either side of a winding stone walkway, creating an inviting, shady entrance. The annual color of pink caladiums works in pleasant contrast to the white house. This planting is changed seasonally by the owner, and varies in variety from year to year.

The rear garden has two main outdoor "rooms." One serves functionally and aesthetically, containing the brick drive; the other is a small courtyard formed by a property wall on the west side and a breezeway that connects the house to the garage.

The brick driveway and breezeway walk feature a herringbone pattern. The mowing strip, which also serves as a walkway in the rear garden, uses a running-bond brick pattern.

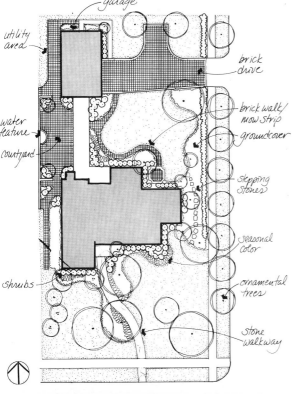

(Top) Herringbone brick paving with cast-stone edge.

(Right) Breezeway with west courtyard beyond.

(Right) Brick drive to coach house.

(Bottom left) Stone walkway to front door.

(Bottom right) Curved walkway mowing strip in a running-bond pattern.

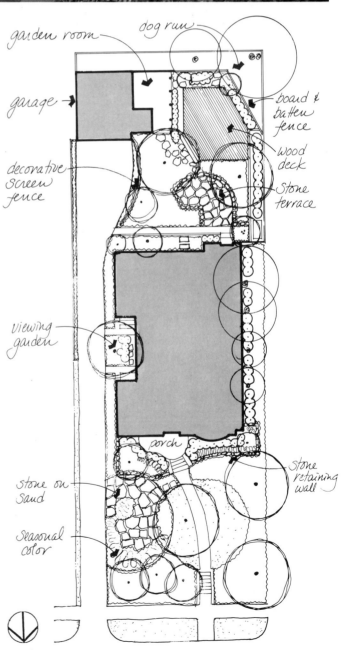

garden room

dog run

garage

board & batten fence

decorative screen fence

wood deck

stone terrace

viewing garden

porch

stone retaining wall

stone on sand

seasonal color

(*Top right*) Front of the house.

(*Top left*) Stone terrace viewed from second-story balcony.

(*Center*) View of rear garden from the back of the house.

(*Bottom*) Wood deck and dog-run fence.

The Author's Original Design Studio

The program requirements of this project, a former residence/office of mine, were complicated. My first design studio was built in the attic; I was working with landscape architects Lee Overstreet and Arpad Pahany at that time. We decided to install as many different kinds of plants as possible here — creating a test lab of sorts — in order to show clients these materials at the office as we discussed their particular landscapes.

My wife Judy was teaching school and I was just starting a new business, so we had very little money to spend for this sort of thing; consequently, we planted small plants and did most of the work ourselves. Although we kept two existing hackberry trees, we also installed several new trees.

As you might imagine, the landscaping of this house/studio quickly became rather overdone, not only because we needed to use so many plants for the lab, but also because I tried a lot of new ideas. I tortured some plants pretty severely and created quite a mess at times.

We also experimented with some hard-construction ideas. One day Arpad and I decided it would be fun to go downstairs, tear out the walls of the maid's quarters (we didn't have a maid anyway), and turn it into a garden room. We thought about it for about 10 seconds, went downstairs, and did it! You can see from the photographs that the open feel works quite nicely with the small garden. The columns were made simply by combining 2x4's and covering them with rough cedar that matched the wood fence.

When we lived here, the area near the dog run was grass; we decided to build a redwood deck right over the very healthy lawn. Not exactly a conventional procedure, but we never had any problems with grass coming through the deck. This installation proved, contrary to popular opinion, that the removal of grass and the installation of plastic or gravel is a total waste of time and money.

Now, let me tell you about dog runs. The one at this house was half gravel, half concrete. The gravel was a maintenance problem, but the concrete proved to be very satisfactory. Since then, I've recommended all-concrete dog runs. The concrete, which is easy to keep clean, also helps to keep the dogs' toenails filed. When building a dog run, it's also a good idea, if possible, to incorporate some adjoining shelter. In this project, a doorway was placed between dog run and garage to allow the dogs to escape from bad weather.

(Top) Redwood deck, bronze furniture, view of garden room.

(Bottom) View from garden room toward house.

Contemporary Use of a Large Lot

A large site always presents special design opportunities. This one featured gentle contours and many existing trees, which provided a beautiful setting for a large house with extensive recreational amenities: swimming pool, tennis court, spa, terraces, and open play areas.

Contemporary architecture isn't exactly plentiful in Texas, but this one is certainly worth mentioning. The circular motor court is flanked by raised brick planters filled with live oak trees and annual plantings (shown here are red geraniums and Asian jasmine ground cover).

Because of the owners' need for privacy, existing trees and large native shrubs around the perimeter of the property were saved. Space was established for a future tennis court in the far northeast corner of the property; it was designed to be as unobtrusive as amenities of that scale can be.

The angular and geometric forms of all site improvements contrast interestingly and pleasantly with the natural setting of the site. Buff-colored brick and exposed aggregate concrete were used for all the terrace areas, retaining walls, steps, and the swimming pool deck. The palette of materials needs to be very simple when the lines and the grade changes vary as much as they do in this garden.

(Top) Steps and wrought-iron rail connecting two terrace levels.

(Center left) Raised planters in front garden area.

(Center right) Pool furniture and deck and coping material.

(Bottom) Raised planter and step transition at pool deck.

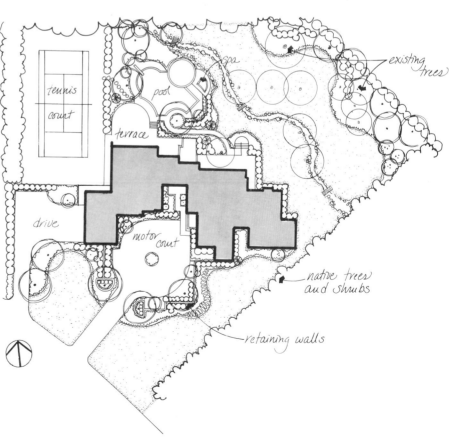

(Top) Front motor court.

(Bottom) View under existing tree to existing plant materials at property line.

existing trees

native trees and shrubs

retaining walls

tennis court

pool

spa

terrace

drive

motor court

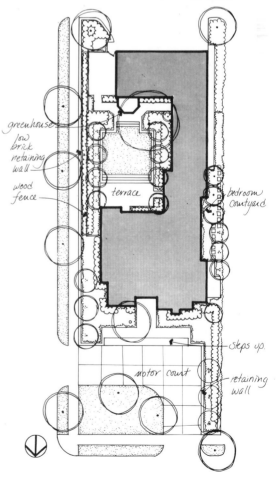

(Top) Rear garden area showing grass, retaining walls and greenhouse.

(Bottom) Utility area, barbecue pit, and trampoline.

greenhouse

low
brick
retaining
wall

wood
fence

terrace

bedroom
courtyard

steps up

motor court

retaining
wall

A Grand Entrance

The need for a circular driveway and front parking space created the main design problem in this project. To make matters worse, this project is located in a city that limits the amount of paving allowed in front yard areas.

Circular driveways should blend aesthetically with the house; in this case, the brick, which establishes the grid pattern in the driveway, is the same as the brick used on the house. The drive and the long, graceful steps flow to the house without appearing to be "tacked on." Although this front area contains enough paving to make it functional, the brick grid effectively reduces the apparent scale of the driveway.

Using a long, narrow planting strip to separate walls from paving is a very effective design detail.

The fence is a board-and-batten design, painted to match the trim on the house; the brick columns are the same type used throughout the rest of the project.

The rear garden consists of a more formal terrace and planting area. A small working greenhouse is the focal point when viewed from the living room; a built-in barbecue area is adjacent to the greenhouse. The play area, situated around the corner from the barbecue, is in a very tightly structured space dominated by a large trampoline.

(Left) Front of house and motor court.

(Bottom left) Close-up of paving system and white brick retaining wall.

(Bottom right) Raised planter, board-and-batten fence with brick columns.

Pathway Through the Trees

Remodeling an existing garden can be easy and a lot of fun if certain things are taken into consideration at the start. This project contained many existing trees, which set the stage for an interesting concept of free-flowing circulation paths and planting.

The existing gravel driveway was retained and enhanced by steel edging. Concrete mowing strips were added to the planting areas to separate the grass from the ground cover and to provide ease of maintenance.

The old horse stable in the rear garden, which now serves as a studio, may be viewed from the main house through an inviting stand of trees. The free-flowing walkway system, which connects the main house to the studio, offers access to the entire garden on a smooth, hard surface of sandblasted, exposed-aggregate concrete.

(Above) Sandblasted concrete walkway system with stable in background.

(Left) View from the house to the entrances at street.

100

(Left) Front of the house and gravel motor court.

(Below) Pecos tan stepping-stones leading to French doors.

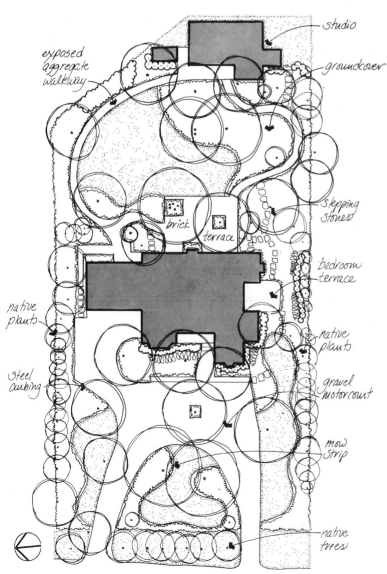

studio

exposed aggregate walkway

groundcover

stepping stones

brick terrace

bedroom terrace

native plants

native plants

steel curbing

gravel motorcourt

mow strip

native trees

101

(Top left) Detail of the steps at the front door, limestone paving and slate risers.

(Top center) Wrought-iron pocket gate.

(Top right) Raised planter and step detail.

(Left) View of swimming pool area with golf course vista in background.

(Bottom) View looking toward the house across the pool.

Preserving the View

Making the garden an architectural extension of the house was the primary goal of this exciting, contemporary project. White limestone and materials of sharply contrasting colors worked together throughout the site.

The planting was kept to a minimum, not only because of the functional requirements of the front motor court, but also because of the magnificent rear-garden views. When a home has a view of one of the most beautiful golf holes in Texas, who needs a lot of planting? Besides the great view, the rear garden features a dark-plastered swimming pool with water feature and a stone terrace throughout.

The front garden is marked by white limestone walls, which act as retainers and privacy screens. The white limestone of the walls matches that of the house. The paving system in the motor court is black Mexican pebble set in concrete. Tennessee gray stone paving strips are used as accents.

(Top) Redwood deck, opaque stained, Tennessee gray stone.

(Center right) Redwood deck.

(Center left) Front view of porte-cochere, crape myrtle.

(Bottom) Side view of porte-cochere showing paving system.

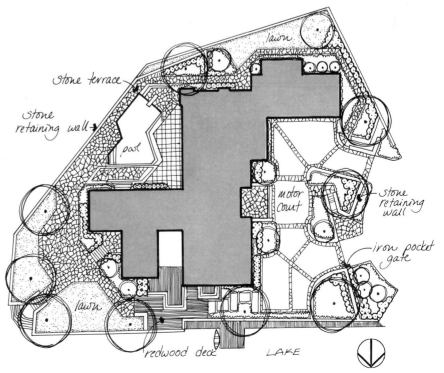

The program here was to incorporate a new swimming-pool area into an old, established, beautiful garden. A new poolhouse was concurrently designed and built by the owner. Coordinating the swimming pool and poolhouse was quite an orchestration, not only because of aesthetic considerations, but also because of the city's set-back requirements.

This natural pool setting features a stone deck, set in a random pattern; a board-and-batten fence with gray, opaque stain; and heavy masses of new planting. The orientation of the pool to the poolhouse makes the circulation and use of the space work easily.

(Top) View of pool area from main house.

(Center) Stone deck, furniture, potted plants, English ivy.

(Bottom) Board-and-batten fence with detailed column and cap.

(Above right) View across the pool to the new poolhouse.

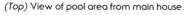

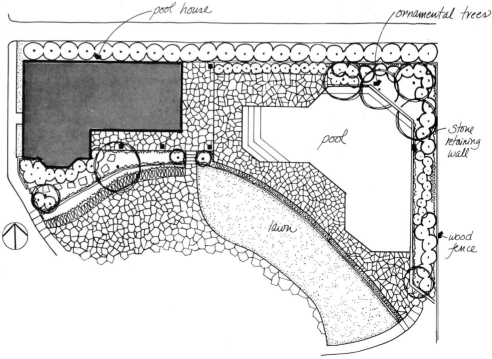

Building a Pool in the Trees

The challenge of this site was designing a swimming pool on a sloped area near a stand of lovely cedar elm trees.

The grade change dictated that the pool be set at an elevation halfway between the home and the creek; still, the pool needed to be as close to the grade of the cedar elms as possible, to retain the soil level at the base of the trees. Maintaining this soil level was essential to ensure the trees' survival.

Incorporating the pool into the grade change was accomplished by using a white stone retaining wall; the result was a pool that was sited without a single tree lost.

The deck is made of exposed aggregate pea-gravel concrete. Finishing touches include Asian jasmine ground cover, accenting wood fern, and massed dwarf shrubs.

(Left) View across pool to house.

(Below) Swimming pool viewed from the house.

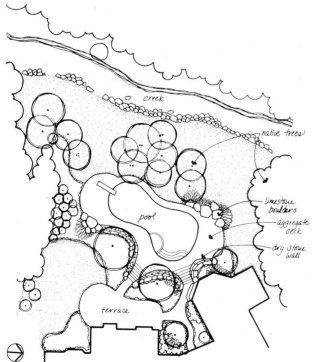

A Striking Lakeside Setting

This unique townhouse, designed by architect Donald Jarvis, is situated effectively on the edge of a small lake. Landscape spaces around and within the townhouse are small but functional.

The paving system in the front is a combination of concrete and brick edging. The paving design allows the driveway and walkway to blend literally and visually, avoiding the boring straight-line driveway effect.

In the rear and interior courtyard, circulation and paving systems are Pecos tan stone set on concrete slabs. Here, the primary design objective was to provide convenient circulation routes and sitting areas from which to view the beautiful lake. The purpose of the interior garden plan was to continue the outdoor feeling indoors, in part by providing the gentle sounds of water that can be heard throughout the house.

(Top left) Under the rear balcony.

(Bottom left) Stone terrace, bench, other furniture, and accessories.

(Right) Townhouse facade.

Opposite Page:

(Top) Interior court at ground level.

(Center) Interior courtyard and water feature seen from second floor.

(Bottom) Stone deck and lake viewed from second-story balcony.

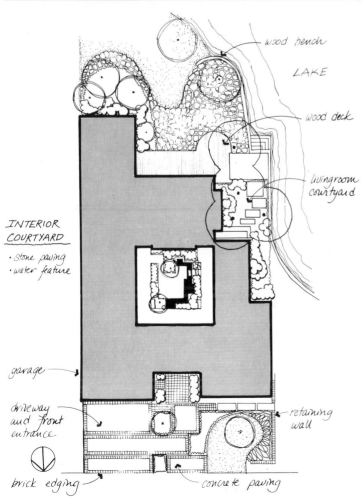

wood bench

LAKE

wood deck

livingroom
courtyard

INTERIOR
COURTYARD
· stone paving
· water feature

garage

driveway
and front
entrance

retaining
wall

brick edging

concrete paving

(*Top*) Front garden showing berms and Asian jasmine.

(*Center left*) Crape myrtles used in the berm system.

(*Center right*) Asian jasmine separates the spa from the swimming pool deck.

(*Bottom*) Driveway area.

Starting with a Bare Site

One of my very first designs, this flat front-yard garden was enclosed and highlighted by the addition of earth berms, Asian jasmine, crape myrtles, live oaks, Bradford pears, and a curving sidewalk. The materials were chosen to provide year-round color and to create an inviting feel from the walkway to the front door.

The swimming pool became the focal point of the rear garden and was set at an elevation of 3 feet below the finished floor of the house and upper terrace. Special care was given to preserve and enhance the natural areas found on two sides of the pool.

A dog run was constructed in such a way that it is hidden in the landscape, but the dog still has a view to the outside.

(Above) Curved-line steel curbing separates Asian jasmine from Bermuda lawn.

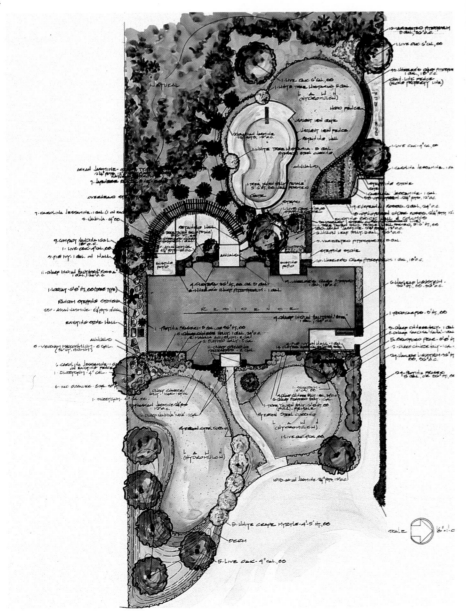

Another early project combines 1930 Tudor architecture with soft planting and specimen trees that frame the main features of the house.

It's important to note here that the beautiful stained-glass window was left unobstructed by large shrubs. One very large existing shrub (pictured on the left), which had grown literally into a tree, was retained. The plant, an arborvitae, is not one we would normally use in a project, but because of its size and health we made a specific effort to retain it as an important design feature of the front garden.

(Left) Front view of the residence in summer.

(Below) Front view of the residence in fall.

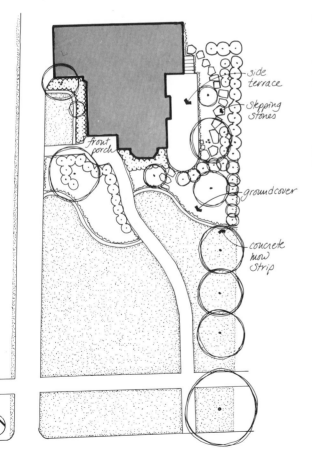

side terrace

stepping stones

front porch

groundcover

concrete mow strip

A Garden in the East Texas Woods

It's great to work on a project that involves existing trees, but such an installation does create special problems. This house, sited to fit gently against the existing trees, had an inconvenient low-drainage area that visitors had to cross before entering the front door. A raised wood-deck pathway, built from the circular drive to the front door, solved this dilemma.

By the swimming pool, the owners wanted to have plenty of room for sun bathing and for growing annuals and perennials. Since the property is very large, with panoramic back yard views, the area was not obstructed by many new plantings.

(Left) Rock drainage area in the front garden.

(Right top) Wood deck at circular drive.

(Right center) Swimming pool area.

(Right bottom) Wood walkway to the front door.

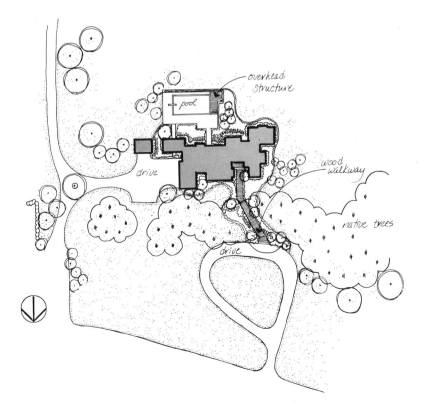

111

Giving the Front Walk a New Twist

This house originally had a ho-hum, typically straight walkway to the front door. Grass flanked the walkway, which led to the predictably straight foundation planting at the house.

The new concept uses a curving sidewalk that varies in width for added visual interest. A curved planting bed displays free-form masses of plant materials. Most of the trees that you see in the photograph were added to the existing trees to complete the scheme.

(Right) Winding sidewalk to the front door.

(Below) Curved ground cover planting bed.

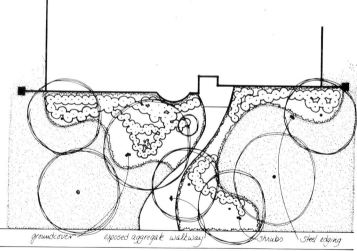

groundcover   exposed aggregate walkway   shrubs   steel edging

Formal Design with Curved Lines

When this home was remodeled, its architecture was made even more formal, so the new landscape concept had to be appropriate. This project shows clearly how formal architecture can be combined with a soft, curving garden. The quality plant materials and the use of red brick give the garden its flavor.

The brick mowing strip blends with the walkway system and architecture, and also serves as a low-maintenance addition to the garden.

(Left) A brick mowing strip separates Asian jasmine beds from the grass.

(Below) Front view showing brick sidewalk and soft foundation planting.

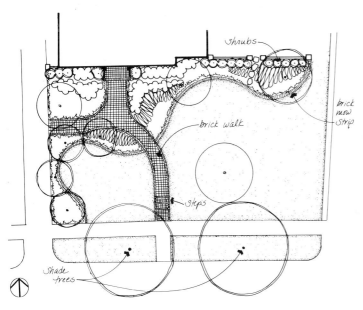

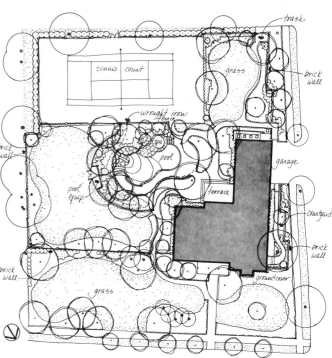

(Top) Curved, removable wrought-iron fence.

(Left) A backdrop of trees separates the pool deck from the children's play area.

114

Child-Proofing the Pool

Two major challenges existed here. The first was designing an unobtrusive tennis court into an exclusive residential area. The tennis court was designed into the rear corner of the property, surrounded by an antique brick wall.

The second request of the owners was for a swimming pool; because of visiting grandchildren, safety considerations were warranted in this area.

Child-proofing a pool completely is impossible; attempts to do so often cause more problems than they solve. Here, however, we found a successful way to deal with the problem. A fence of removable iron panels was constructed around the pool to provide safety when necessary, and an unobstructed view when the grandchildren are not in residence.

It's interesting to note that there were no existing trees in this back garden; trees were introduced to form attractive backdrops and provide shade in certain areas of the swimming-pool deck.

Another important facet of this garden is the swimming-pool diving board; it was built flush with a raised area of the deck. In general, I feel that swimming-pool accessories should be kept to a minimum. Items such as ladders, diving boards, and slides should be avoided if possible.

(Left) Curved walk to tennis court using brick columns and brown/black fencing.

(Right top) Raised deck area at the diving board, brass drain grate and skimmer cover in the foreground.

(Right bottom) Antique brick wall, Asian jasmine in the foreground, Boston ivy on the wall.

Plant Small Trees and Let Them Grow

This project was designed on scratch paper at the client's house; later, they installed the project from the sketch shown on this page. The house originally had large, overgrown shrubs that masked the pleasant lines of the house.

The new design incorporates curving lines, fast-growing cedar elm, and pistachio trees planted in key spots. Asian jasmine ground cover, paired with just the right splash of seasonal color, makes the front entry a pleasing, appropriate facade for this English cottage.

(Right) Overall front view of the house.

(Below) Close-up of the curved ground cover bed.

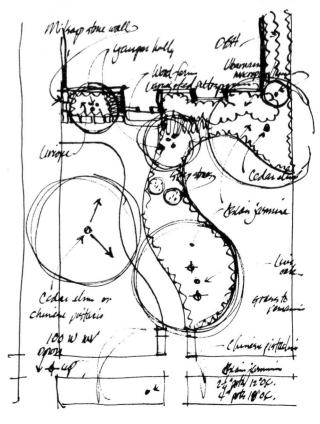

Small Site with Large Grade Change

This was the first house for a young, single businessman who wanted to swim, relax, and entertain on a casual basis. The house sat on a steeply sloped lot. Because of this grade change, especially in the front yard, the walk and steps were built to curve gracefully up the hill, stop at a landing, then continue to the house. Trees were used as the major planting elements, along with a simple foundation planting and border for the walkway.

The pool area and rear garden are compact and efficient; materials are subtle and of high quality: no plastic skimmer covers or drain inlets, no coolcrete deck, no flashy ceramic frostline tile. The deck is sandblasted, exposed aggregate concrete.

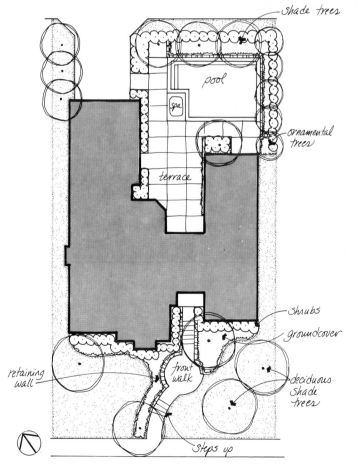

(Top) Front garden with landing at midpoint of winding entrance walk.

(Bottom) Swimming pool in the rear garden.

Pools Are For More Than Swimming

Adding a swimming pool to a small rear garden was the objective here.

The pool area was designed with crisp, straight lines and high-quality materials to create a clean, elegant design statement. You'll see no diving board, metal ladders, or windmills around this pool. The planting plan is also very simple.

The construction materials used were Tennessee gray limestone for the deck, dark gray slate for the frost line tile, and gray-green plaster for the swimming pool. All drain inlets and skimmer covers are brass, rather than the typical, inferior, white plastic. The furniture is bronze Walter Lamb.

The solid side fence was designed to appear as a decorative screen rather than a solid fence. The illusion of depth is created by rough cedar 2x2s, painted a light color and backed by a solid, dark-gray fence.

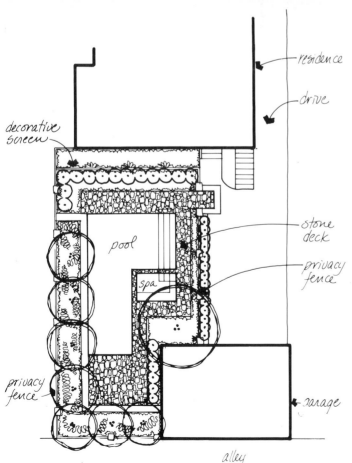

(*Above*) Pool, decorative screen in distance, and privacy fence to the right.

(*Top left*) View of swimming pool from the house.

Creating an Effect with Trees

This project, which started out as a bare front yard, was designed to create the impression that the house had been built among existing trees. This was accomplished by adding live oaks and red oaks in an asymmetrical way, avoiding the typical frame-the-front-door concept. The trees were allowed to grow naturally. Lower tree limbs were not trimmed excessively, nor were the trees cut into symmetrical shapes; both are fairly typical pruning errors. The overall soft-and-simple planting plan uses low-maintenance plant materials.

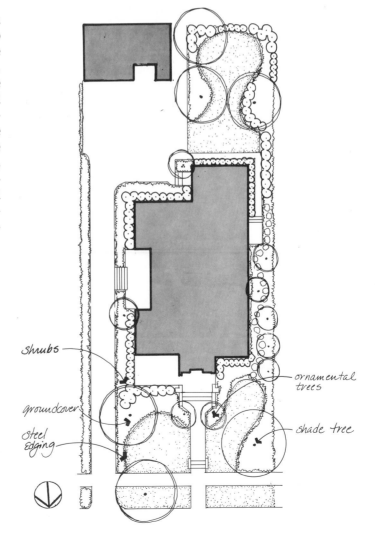

shubs

groundcover

steel edging

ornamental trees

shade tree

119

Low-maintenance Townhouse Courtyards

The front area needed to easily accommodate cars entering from a busy street. The other main objective was to design three low-maintenance courtyards that would be pleasant to view from indoors throughout the various seasons.

The front motor court is constructed of exposed aggregate concrete; the front planting is primarily Asian jasmine around the existing slash pine trees, highlighted by azaleas, wood fern, and variegated pittosporum.

The east courtyard features a stone-on-sand terrace, ophiopogon ground cover, azaleas, a Japanese maple understory tree, and clematis vines on the wood fence. The center courtyard employs a brick paving system with spaces in the brick for very simple plantings; the brick is set at an angle to help create the illusion of a slightly larger courtyard. A main objective of this central area was to keep the existing crape myrtle tree in its original location. The simple west courtyard uses ophiopogon in the small planting areas around existing trees.

(Right) Middle courtyard's brick paving system, crape myrtle, and hibiscus.

Opposite page:

(Top) Overall view of the front garden.

(Bottom right) West courtyard features a stone-on-sand paving system.

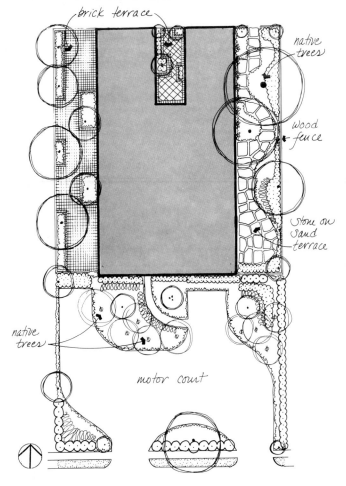

brick terrace

native trees

wood fence

stone on sand terrace

native trees

motor court

(Top) Spa in wood deck with cover removed.

(Bottom left) A view across the stone-on-sand terrace to the board-and-batten fence.

(Bottom right) Upper-level wood deck with light, contemporary furniture.

Protecting the Trees with a Wood Deck

Working around several beautiful existing trees was the main challenge in this small area. The design solution was to build the circulation system via multilevel wood decks and stone-on-sand paths, which do not disturb the root systems of nearby trees.

Finishing touches in this very private rear garden include simple garden furniture and a spa, installed with a convenient removable cover.

(Left) A view across the stone-on-sand terrace to the board-and-batten fence.

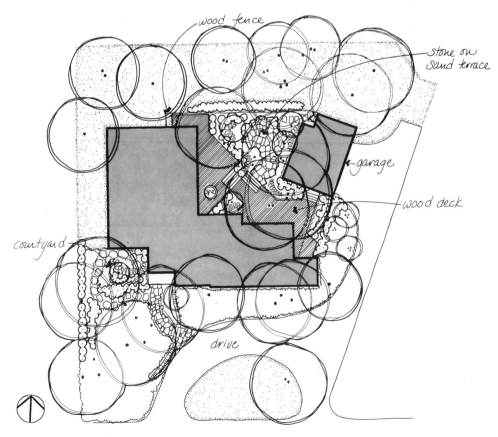

Expanding the Terrace

The classic architecture of this home dictated that the front garden's design remain very simple; a plus was being able to take advantage of the magnificent existing trees. This is a project where typical foundation planting is appropriate. A new walkway was added from the driveway to the front porch, which blended with the existing walkway that bisected the front lawn.

An existing rear patio was demolished to make room for the spacious brick terrace with two distinct sitting areas. New doors were added to the den of the house, offering access to the side portion of the terrace.

In the rear, behind the new driveway, a utility garden was added; here, the owners grow vegetables, cut flowers, and herbs.

(Left) Utility garden area near the garage.

(Below) Overall front view.

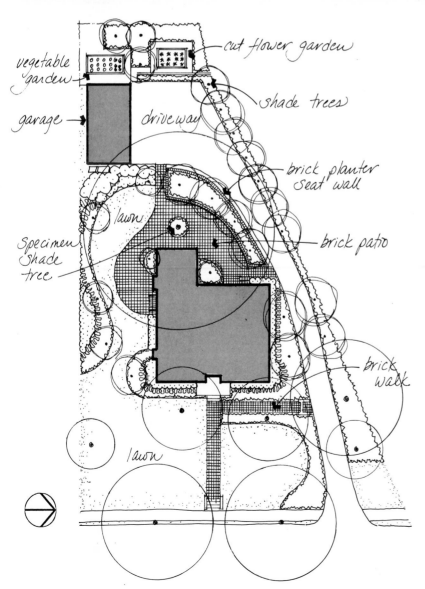

vegetable garden

cut flower garden

garage

driveway

shade trees

brick planter seat wall

lawn

Specimen shade tree

brick patio

brick walk

lawn

(Top) View from the rear terrace to the utility area.

(Bottom right) Rear garden along the south side of the residence.

An Atypical Entrance Walk

(Right) Overall view of the front.

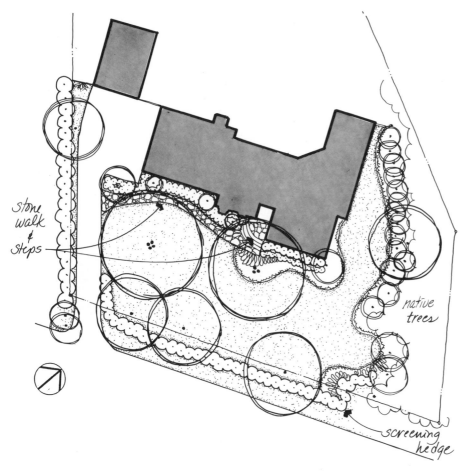

stone
walk
&
steps

native
trees

screening
hedge

A common request was encountered here: The owner wanted a new walkway connecting the driveway to the front door. The typical way to handle this is to run a straight walk near the house to a set of square stairs — a predictable solution. Instead, the walkway was designed to terminate into curved steps in a meandering fashion; the entire system was constructed of Pennsylvania green stone set on a 4-inch concrete slab. The flowing lines of the new walkway maximized the long, dramatic lines of the house.

New planting consisted of dwarf Chinese holly in masses, azaleas, wood fern, Japanese maple, and crape myrtles.

Planting Honors Window Design

The primary goal of this design was a planting plan that would respect the architecture of this fine old home. Notice how the shrub planting honors the window detailing, and how the overused straight-line foundation-planting concept has been intentionally avoided.

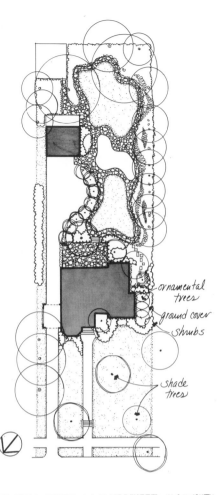

ornamental trees

ground cover shrubs

shade trees

(Above) Foundation planting and window detail.

(Right) Overall view of the house.

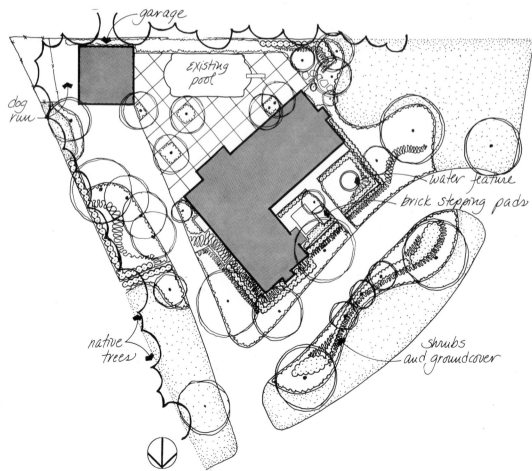

garage

existing
pool

dog
run

water feature

brick stepping pads

native
trees

shrubs
and groundcover

Lighting Completes the Design

This client wanted a lush setting to come home to after work every day. Although the style of the house might suggest a formal and structured landscape plan, the solution here is quite different. Instead, we devised flowing masses of various plants that would provide permanent color on a seasonal basis, along with areas of annual flowers.

From a design standpoint, circular driveways bother me. Since we encountered an existing circular driveway here, we designed the planting scheme to maximize the ornamental vegetation and minimize the driveway.

The lighting design plays an important role in the overall scheme, and allows the garden to be enjoyed night and day.

Another interesting feature of this project is the dog run. It seems that the best dog run design consists of a compact space, plain concrete with a lightly brushed finish, and chain-link fencing painted a dark color. (Sometimes bird dogs need a chain-link roof to prevent them from jumping out of the area.)

(Opposite page) Garden at night.

(Left) A look at the circular driveway.

(Below) Overall view of the front of the house.

(Top) Illumination of rear garden.

(Center left) East side garden using pencil rock and existing plant material.

(Center right) Entrance walk.

(Bottom left) Greek pot backed by native shrubs.

(Bottom right) Overall view of the front garden.

Opposite page:

(Left) West Oriental garden.

(Right) Curved stone-on-sand walkway to gazebo.

The Author's Current Experimental Lab

In the front yard, we needed a sidewalk to provide access from the driveway to the front door. Therefore, a crushed-granite walkway of varying widths was added; ground covers of mock strawberry and English ivy were installed for visual softness. Outside the dining room, heavy plant materials were used so that, ultimately, the dining room will be screened off from the street. A heavy grove of red oak trees was added to encircle the property, in anticipation of a motor court to be added to the center of the front yard.

The back yard's small pond, filled with aquatic plants and Japanese koi, is an exposed aggregate concrete shell. The aquatic plants are cyperus, horsetail, dwarf aquatic bamboo, and lotus.

This, my current experimental lab, is in the first phases of installation; as usual, I'm trying a lot of new ideas, such as water features that are economical to install and reasonable to maintain. The Oriental water feature, a basin and bamboo flume, employs a submerged pump and a fiberglass bowl under the Tejas river pebbles.

This garden featured large existing trees along the east and north sides of the property; new trees were added along the west side to provide shade from the afternoon sun.

The stone-on-sand walkway system in the back was designed to act as an edging and as a walkway system connecting the upper terrace swimming-pool area to the gazebo, the focal point in the far corner of the garden.

The dog run and utility area merge with the central circulation system in the landscape. There's also enough storage space in the dog run area for wheelbarrows, garden tools, compost, and firewood.

In the east courtyard, near the master bedroom, stones have been laid vertically to act as sculpture and stepping stones; vertical stones complete the look of this small garden.

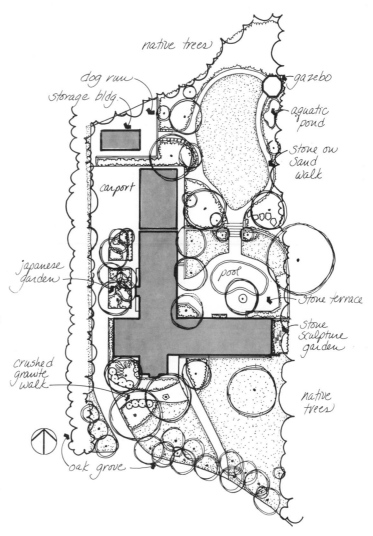

Capturing Off-Site Views

This property had two major existing amenities. One, in the front yard, was a stand of small cedar elm trees located near the street; the other was a greenbelt in the back yard. The client wanted a convenient entrance area, a swimming pool with plenty of terrace and deck for entertaining, and a workable utility area.

Introducing the new walkway and entrance into the existing stand of cedar elms was handled by using a short retaining wall to maintain the grade at the base of the elms. A round, raised planter was added opposite the cedar elms for balance; a yaupon holly tree was also installed. At the time of the home's construction, the cedar elms were about 6 feet tall; they've now grown into important visual elements in the front garden.

In the rear, the pool sits near the house, working with dramatically curving steps that connect the pool to the upper terrace. The entire deck affords a view to the greenbelt area through the open wrought-iron fence. The space outside the fence serves as an excellent location for the clients' perennial-color garden.

(Right) Curved steps at swimming pool.

(Bottom left) Through the existing cedar elms to the front door.

(Bottom right) View to greenbelt and perennial garden through wrought-iron fence.

Opposite page:

(Top) Overall view of the front garden.

(Bottom right) Raised planter for annuals at front door.

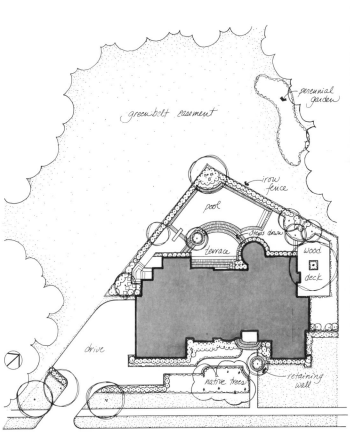

133

When we began this project, we encountered a stained and cracked coolcrete deck that had been covered with artificial grass. The decision was made to remove and redo everything on the site except for the pool shell and selected plant materials. Thus, we added a paving system of gridded concrete, a poolhouse, a circular driveway of sandblasted exposed-aggregate concrete, free-form planting areas, and trees.

Another significant part of the design was the solution of a drainage problem at the back of the house; we did this by using PVC and gravel (an underground French-type drain). The system circles the east side of the house, and exits through the curb at the front of the house.

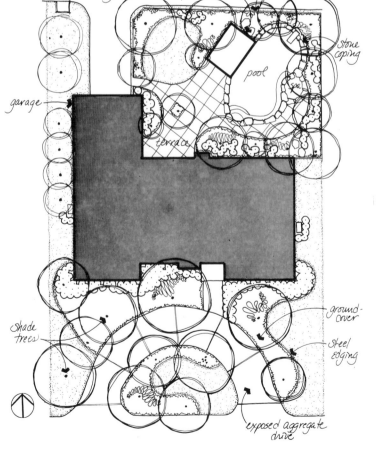

(Top) The front garden's driveway and planting.

(Center) View from the new garden room to the residence.

(Bottom) New paving system and planting.

An O'Neil Ford Home — Revitalized

(Left) Close-up view of the house and simple foundation planting of dwarf Chinese holly and English Ivy and the front garden's grassy expanse.

The program here was to return this O'Neil Ford designed home to its original splendor. The new landscape scheme uses a simple and elegant design.

We kept the existing trees intact; removed a long, streetside hedge that blocked the view of the house; and added large, free-flowing beds of English ivy ground cover around the trees on both sides of the house. The ornamental trees flanking the front door are coral bark Japanese maples. All low shrubbery is dwarf Chinese holly.

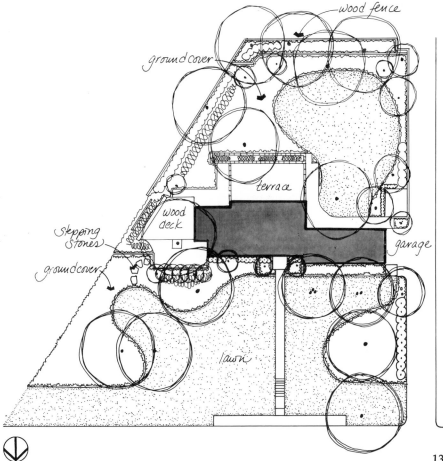

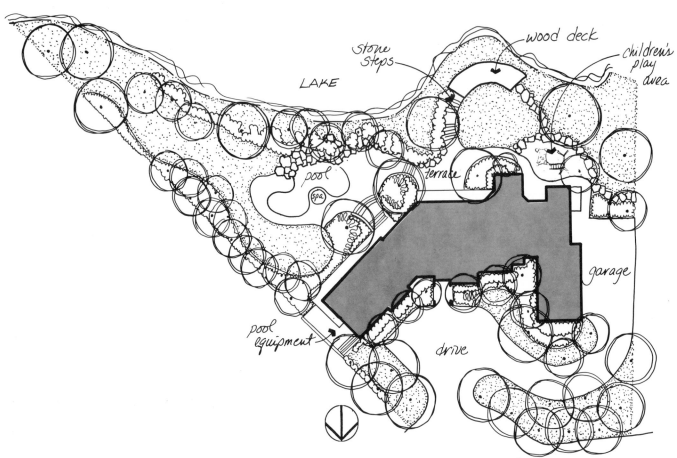

LAKE

stone steps

wood deck

children's play area

pool

spa

terrace

garage

pool equipment

drive

Stone Gardens

The project involved a large house built on the edge of a small lake, with very little room for needed children's play areas, entertainment terraces, a swimming pool, water features, and a sun-bathing area.

The house was built of white limestone, so a light-colored limestone theme became the primary material for all new hard construction elements. New and existing features were blended by using large limestone boulders, retaining walls, and paving. A redwood deck was constructed at the water's edge primarily to save large existing bur oak trees.

The apparent size and scale of the rear garden was effectively enlarged by the use of several outdoor "rooms," created by grade changes, limestone rock, and plant materials. The large grass area on the far end of the property gives the illusion of spaciousness.

The free-form pool has the look of a natural pond. The limestone rock outcropping, covered with plants, serves as a water feature and as the basis for the grade change; here, plantings screen views of the pool area to allow sun-bathing privacy.

The lake edge defines the property line on one side; a very simple, 1x2 board fence is the northern property line boundary. Several new trees — including additional bur oaks — were added to the scheme for shade on the southwest side of the house.

(Opposite page) Overall view of the residence.

(Left) Wrought-iron fence with welded wire at children's play area.

(Right) Redwood deck and furniture.

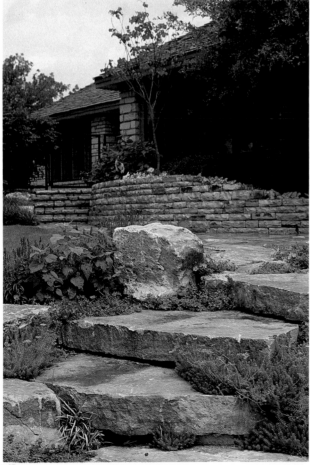

(Top) Transition area from wood deck to floor level of residence.

(Bottom left) Stone steps.

(Bottom right) Overall view of the swimming-pool area.

Opposite page:

(Top left) Therapy pool separated from the main pool body.

(Top right) Limestone retaining wall and paving system.

(Left center) Water feature at swimming pool, canvas umbrella, and contemporary furniture.

(Bottom) Pool area's limestone paving system and redwood furniture.

Commercial Design

The same thought process of creating pleasant garden spaces applies to residential *and* commercial projects. Commercial projects are much like residential projects except that they are larger and, sometimes, more conceptual (have fewer small details). Too, commercial projects are usually viewed from a distance, while residential projects are more often scrutinized up close. Commercial projects, in particular, need to look close to their best from the beginning, to increase the marketability of the property.

The first commercial projects I did in Dallas have turned out pretty well — considering I had no idea what I was doing. Today our projects are based primarily on tested and proven methods, although we continue to stay on the cutting edge of innovation. In other words, we come up with a lot of wild ideas — and most of them work!

Junior League of Dallas Headquarters

(Left) Angular view of the front, showing the surrounding planting.

(Opposite page, bottom) The headquarters and motor court.

The project needed a pastoral effect but had to be formal enough to blend with the surrounding traditional residential neighborhood.

For the motor court and front terrace, we used a combination of dark brick pavers and panels of exposed aggregate concrete.

Cedar elm trees were used in the parking lot to lessen the expanse of concrete paving. The wall system around the property line was constructed of the same stucco as the building.

The building architect was Beran & Shelmire Architects.

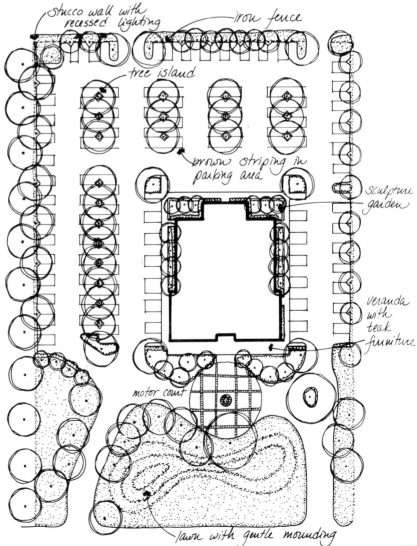

stucco wall with recessed lighting

iron fence

tree island

brown striping in parking area

sculpture garden

veranda with teak furniture

motor court

lawn with gentle mounding

141

One Main Place

This design involved the remodeling of an existing rooftop landscape; being the rooftop of a subterranean parking garage, the plaza-level landscape is actually *below* street level. The plaza level had some leakage problems, structural limitations, and an existing water feature that rarely worked.

A new granite-chip paving system, using terrazo strips, was designed to form the paving grid. Raised tree planters were designed in two different depths; cedar elms were planted in 36-inch-deep planters, and yaupon hollies in 18-inch-deep planters. Liriope was used for ground cover; various annuals are used on a year-round basis.

The owner is RREEF Funds; the original architect was SOM; and the architect for the renovation project was HKCP.

(Right) Overall view, looking down from the street level.

(Below) At plaza level, looking through the planters.

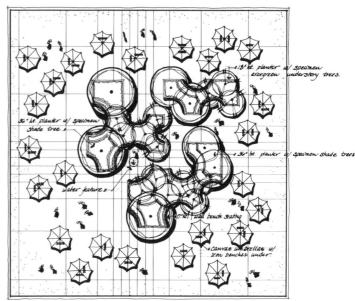

142

5401 Central

This job featured the first known commercial use of an unusual tree called the pond cypress (Taxodium ascendens). The planting scheme is simple but distinctive to flatter the low glass building designed by Rosetti Associates. The grass is common Bermuda; the shrubs along the base of the building are elaeagnus. For the west side of the building, cedar elms were selected, along with dwarf Chinese holly and Asian jasmine for the base of the building.

(Above) Back side of building features pond cypresses and grass.

(Right) Front of the building features cedar elm trees.

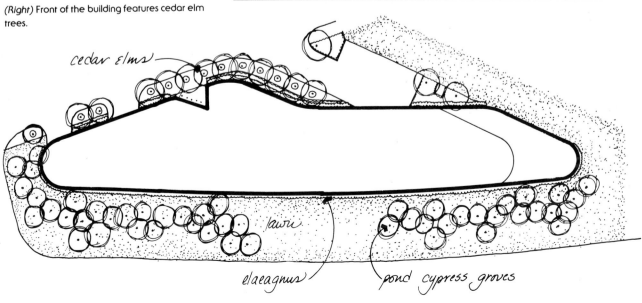

cedar elms

lawn

elaeagnus

pond cypress groves

American Airlines

Rolling hills, sandy soil, and an abundance of indigenous trees were encountered on this project, a natural environment that called for preserving some elements, and taming others. Working around existing trees is always a difficult situation, but here it was particularly critical. The trees were growing in sandy soil amid the construction of several new buildings.

Large natural "courtyards" were preserved by retaining all the existing plant materials and rock outcroppings. Drainage was routed around the area to discourage erosion of the natural setting.

New plantings, added in the cafeteria area, were more formal and structured, to create an interesting transition from the dramatic architecture to the natural landscape setting.

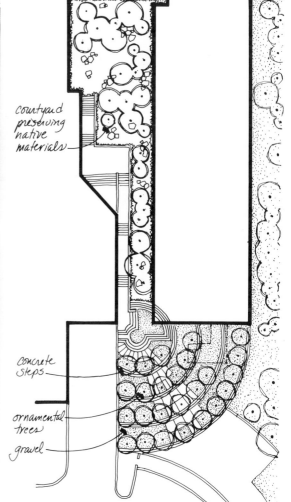

courtyard preserving native materials

concrete steps

ornamental trees

gravel

(Top) "Courtyards" left in a natural condition.

(Bottom) More formal planting at the cafeteria transition area.

144

Diamond Shamrock Tower

A canyonlike feel existed between this office tower and the parking garage across the street. The introduction of the light-colored, lacy, bald cypress trees has created a very popular outdoor space in this once sterile setting. Shade trees encourage people to eat and relax here, even in the summer months. The architect of the project was JPJ Architects.

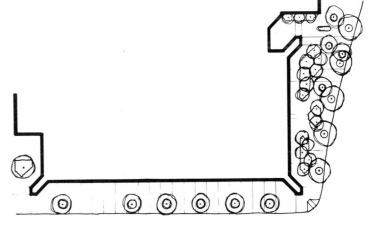

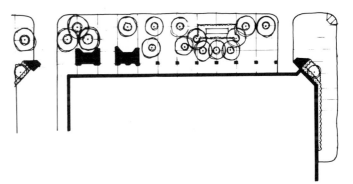

(Top) The dining area and cypress trees.

(Bottom) Overall view of the bald cypress planting at the outdoor restaurant near the parking structure.

(Above) Brick paving system and water feature in the distance.

(Left) Curved 18-inch retaining wall system and planting.

(Opposite page) Overall view from adjacent building.

InterFirst I Roof Garden

Structural limitations, drainage problems, and exaggerated weather conditions make the design of a roof garden among the most difficult of landscape projects. This particular job, situated on the ninth floor of a downtown building, required the selection of hardy plantings able to withstand and thrive in shallow soil and weather extremes; all trees are yaupon hollies, selected for their tolerance to such conditions.

The paving and wall systems, although designed in an interesting free-flowing manner, were made entirely of one material — a dark brown brick — to simplify the hard construction of the garden.

The entire garden is at the same soil depth, 18 inches, which was the maximum amount the structural engineers would allow; this soil depth also simplifies the maintenance of the garden. The project was designed in conjunction with architects Dahl Braden/PTM, Inc.

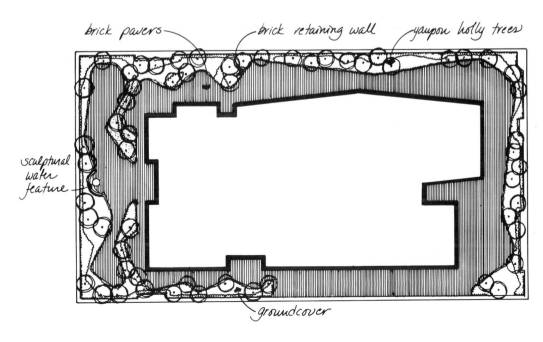

brick pavers

brick retaining wall

yaupon holly trees

sculptural water feature

groundcover

Harris Corporation

The Harris Corporation, one of my earliest commercial projects, was a very large site that needed to be enhanced on a limited budget. The project was broken into three contracts, one for the trees only, the second for the rest of the landscaping including shrubs, ground cover, grass, and irrigations, and the third included the earth work and lighting.

The flat existing site was improved greatly with the addition of free-flowing grass berms. Native trees were used extensively in the grass areas and in the parking lot to diminish the expanse of paving.

This project is a good example of the advantages of backfilling trees with existing soil, rather than using improved mixes.

Architects — Dahl Braden/PTM, Inc.

(Above) Dwarf crape myrtle in foreground; shade trees behind soften the look of the parking area.

(Right) Overall view of the front showing native trees and dwarf red crape myrtle.

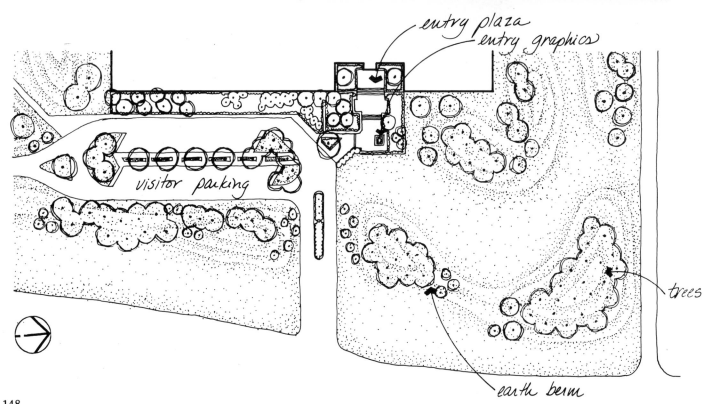

First City Center

It was a challenge to create an urban garden in this setting, a multi-level plaza that doubles an an overstructure for parking areas, truck terminals, and retail shops. Structural complexities were numerous.

Dramatic design elements, including granite steps and retaining walls, a 90-foot granite waterwall with adjoining fountain features, sheltered seating areas, and huge specimen trees, transformed the open space into a pleasant "people place."

Architects — WZMH, Habib.

(Above) Water feature and new cedar elm trees in plaza.

(Left) Raised planter with sweetgums and annual color.

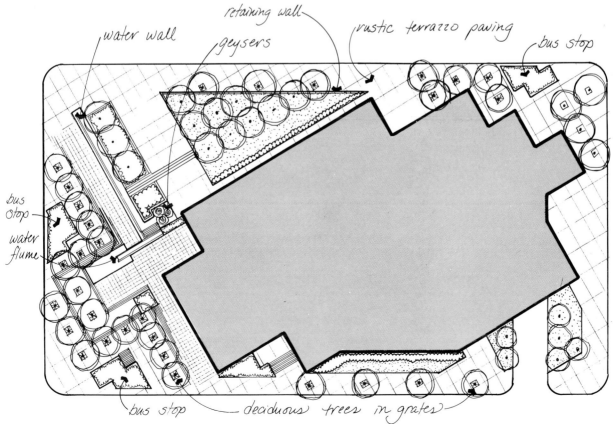

water wall

retaining wall

geysers

rustic terrazzo paving

bus stop

bus stop

water flume

bus stop — deciduous trees in grates

Glossary

ACID, ALKALINE — Descriptions of soil or water pH, 7 being neutral. A pH above 7 indicates alkalinity, and a pH less than 7 indicates acidity. For example, the sandy soils of East Texas are acid, and the clay soils of central and west Texas are alkaline.

ANNUAL — A plant that blooms the first year, then dies.

BACKFILL — Earth used to fill trenches or holes.

BALLED AND BURLAPPED — Tree roots dug with a ball of earth, then wrapped with burlap cloth. The process used for moving larger trees.

BED PREPARATION — Mixing sand and/or organic material with native soil to improve the plant bed.

BIENNIAL — A plant that blooms the second year, then dies.

BOB-BACK — To severely cut back, dehorn, or otherwise brutalize trees.

BUDGET — A mystical number that is supposed to represent the amount of money spent on the landscape.

BURN — Scottish term for creek.

CABLING — Connecting limbs of trees together with steel cable to attempt to prevent ice storm damage.

CALIPER — The diameter of a tree trunk.

CAMBIUM LAYER — The green, life-supporting layer just under the bark of woody plants.

CHLOROSIS — Iron deficiency with visible symptoms of yellow leaves with green veins.

COLLAR — A small stub left on the tree from a pruning cut.

CONCEPTUAL DESIGN — Rough design showing the general location and shape of all the elements in a landscape plan.

CONIFER — A cone bearing, needle leafed plant.

CONSTRUCTION DOCUMENTS — Final drawings and written specifications that are used by contractors to build projects.

COOLCRETE — The poorest quality pool-decking material made. It's supposed to be cooler on bare feet, but the material stains and falls apart so badly it shouldn't even be considered.

CRUSHED GRANITE — Pea-sized granite chips used in paving.

CULTIVATION — Lightly tilling bare soil areas around plants which allows water and air to the root systems.

CUT FLOWER GARDEN — A utility garden area used specifically for growing flowers to cut and bring into the house.

DECIDUOUS — Any plant that dies back or sheds all leaves in the winter and returns in the spring.

DEHORNING — Severely cutting back limbs of trees; butchery.

EVERGREEN — Any plant that stays green year-round.

FLUSH CUT — A pruning cut to remove a tree limb; this cut is completely flush with the trunk. A very bad practice.

FOUNDATION PLANTING — Shrub or ground cover planting used to hide the grade beam of the house.

GARDEN — The proper term for landscaped area or yard.

GERMINATION — The opening and sprouting of a plant seed.

GRADE — The height of garden elements related to each other.

GRADE ADJUSTMENT — Making changes to existing grades.

HARD CONSTRUCTION — The wood, concrete, brick, and other non-living parts of a landscape installation.

HT. — An abbreviation for plant height.

HYDROMULCH — A grass application process which blows the grass seed or sprigs mixed with water and mulch directly onto bare soil.

LANDSCAPE ARCHITECT — *Webster's New Collegiate Dictionary* defines this as: "One whose profession is the arrangement of land for human use and enjoyment involving the placement of structures, vehicular and pedestrian ways, and plantings."

LANDSCAPE ARCHITECTURE — The design of outdoor space and its elements.

LANDSCAPE CONTRACTOR — A company or person performing landscape installation.

LANDSCAPER — No such thing!

MULCH — Material placed on top of the soil that serves to reduce or pre-

150

vent weed growth, insulate soil, reduce moisture loss, and enhance the appearance of the bed. Peat moss, compost, bark, sawdust, straw, and leaves are examples of mulch.

O.C. — On center; this refers to the spacing of planted material.

ORNAMENTAL TREE — A small tree rather than a shade tree. They are used as understory trees or in a mass in the open for color or interesting texture.

PERENNIAL — Plants that return each year in the spring from winter dormancy.

PERGOLA — Another fancy word for overhead structure.

PICK PRUNING — The careful selection of limbs to be removed from plants. The opposite of shearing.

PIER HOLE — A narrow hole dug vertically.

POSITIVE DRAINAGE — Surface or underground drainage that removes excess water.

PRUNING — The removal of limbs and/or foliage from plants.

PVC SLEEVES (Polyvinylchloride plastic) — Plastic pipe used for irrigation, drainage, and other utilities that act as conduit for final piping.

RISERS — The vertical surfaces of steps.

SHADE TREE — Larger trees whose canopies shade the ground plane of a garden.

SHARP SAND — Sand, washed clean of soil, weed, seed, etc.

SPACING — Distance between the center of one plant and the center of the next one.

SPECIMEN TREE — A beautiful or interesting tree that is pleasant or exciting to look at by itself.

SPRIGS — Small pieces of the grass plant used for planting. These pieces are called stolons, which are stems between the leaves and roots.

STAKING — The practice of using ugly poles, stakes, wire, and nails to hold up newly planted trees.

SURFACE DRAINAGE — Surface grading that allows surface water to drain by gravity.

TERRACE — The more proper, but snobby, name for patio. The terrace is actually the entire outdoor paving system.

TIF — Name for the series of hybridized Bermuda grasses.

TIME SCHEDULE — A fictitious term used in the landscape industry to state when the job will be completed.

TREADS — The horizontal surface of steps.

TREE WRAPPING — The art of wrapping cloth or paper around trees to make customers think that their tree trunks have been protected.

UNDER DRAINAGE — Underground, French-type drainage systems that use plastic pipe set in gravel.

UNDERSTORY TREE — A smaller tree that is planted under the canopy of large shade trees.

XERISCAPE — The new buzzword meaning sound landscape practices that promote water conservation.

Index

A

B

C

D

S

sage, green, 51
sago palm. *See* palm, sago
St. Augustine grass. *See* grass, St. Augustine
Sambucus mexicana. See elder, Mexican
San Angelo, Texas, 43, 50
San Antonio, Texas, 43, 49, 54
San Antonio Botanical Center, 49
Savannah holly. *See* holly, Savannah
sawtooth oak. *See* oak, sawtooth
schedule, installation, 9
screen, decorative, 118
sculpture, garden, 83
sculpture, stones as, 83, 131
sedum, 75, 77
senecia, 49, 50, 51, 71, 73
shrubs, 26, 27, 40, 69-73
Siberian elm. *See* elm, Siberian
silver-lace vine, 44, 50, 76, 77
site analysis, 9-10
Six Flags Over Texas, 46
slash pine. *See* pine, slash
snapdragon, 78, 80
soil, 10, 32, 40
SOM (architects), 142
Sophora secundiflora. See laurel, Texas mountain
spas, 21, 36, 96, 108, 122, 123
specifications, 21
sprinkler systems, 27
spirea, 71, 73
stable, 100
stepping stones, 101, 131
steps, 31, 96, 102, 117, 138, 149
storage space, 11, 12, 131
strawberry, mock, 75, 77, 131
streams, 36
structures, overhead, 32, 33
sumac, 35, 46, 62, 67, 71, 73
sun bathing area, 137
swans, 83
sweetgum, 35, 46, 52, 62, 67, 149
swimming pools. *See* pools, swimming
sycamore, 68

T

tallow, Chinese, 68
Taxodium ascendens. See cypress, pond
Taxodium distichum. See cypress, bald
tennis courts, 8, 26, 27, 37, 96, 115
terraces, 12, 29-30; brick, 124; concrete, 27; entertainment, 137; expansion of, 124; stone, 94, 96, 99, 103, 106, 109, 120, 122, 123, 131, 132, 141
Texas A&M University, 2
Texas mountain laurel. *See* laurel, Texas mountain
Texas State Capitol, 49
Texas Tech University, 2, 44
thrift, 78, 80
tif grass. *See* grass, tif
Tom Green County Courthouse, 50

Town Lake area, 49
trampoline, 98, 99
transplanting, 41
trees, 51, 52-68; cabling of, 89; as design tools, 52; endurance of, 4; existing, 27-28; fencing off of, 68; importance of, 4, 27-28; as investments, 26; location of, 14; ornamental, 14; painting cuts of, 68; planting of, 38-40; protection of, 28; pruning of, 4, 68; not recommended, 68; roots of, 9, 27-28, 38, 39, 40, 41, 68; shade, 14, 26; staking of, 40; tips regarding, 68; wrapping of, 40
trellises, 32
trumpet vine, 45, 46, 49, 50, 76, 77
tulip, 78, 80
turtles, 83
Turtle Creek, 46
Turtle Creek Boulevard, 54
Tyler, Texas, 43, 46
Tyler Courthouse, 46
Tyler Rose Gardens, 46

U

Ulmus crassifolia. See elm, cedar
Ulmus parvifolia. See elm, Chinese
umbrella plants, 35
Upper Valley neighborhood (El Paso), 51
University of Texas at Arlington, 2
University of Texas at El Paso, 51
utilities, 21
utility area, 12, 22, 98, 125, 131, 132

V

verbena, 78, 80; best areas in Texas for growing of, 44, 45, 46, 47, 49, 50, 51
viburnum, 47, 71, 73
Victoria, Texas, 43, 47
vinca major, 50
vines, 40, 74-77
Virginia creeper, 44, 45, 50, 76, 77

W

Waco, Texas, 43, 46
walkways, 11, 12, 30, 31, 109, 124, 131, 132; brick, 113; concrete, 22, 100, 106; garden, 27; stone, 92, 93, 126, 131; winding, 92, 93, 110, 112, 117; wood, 111
walls, 27, 32, 36, 99, 147; brick, 33, 37, 115; courtyard, 33; limestone, 33, 103, 139; retaining, 32, 33, 37, 96, 98, 99, 103, 132, 137, 139, 146, 149; screening, 32; stucco, 141
Washingtonia robusta. See palm, Washington
Washington palm. *See* palm, Washington
water, 10, 34, 35
water features, 36, 103, 131, 137, 139, 146, 149
water oak. *See* oak, water
water systems, 27
watering, 40, 90
wax ligustrum. *See* ligustrum, wax
White Rock Creek area, 57

XYZ

*H*oward Garrett is a landscape architect whose firm, Howard Garrett and Associates, has designed and overseen the installation of many of the finest gardens in Texas. His first book, *Plants of the Metroplex,* is considered a valuable reference on plant materials even beyond the area for which it was originally written. A native Texan from Pittsburg in East Texas, Garrett is a graduate of Texas Tech University. His professional experience includes landscape contracting, landscape maintenance, golf course maintenance, and the retail garden shop and nursery business. He lives in Dallas with his wife Judy and daughter Logan.